Treasure Up the Word

Treasure Up the Word

Jay E. Jensen

Bookcraft
Salt Lake City, Utah

Library of Congress Catalog Card Number: 97–74880

ISBN 1–57008–335–5

First Printing, 1997

Printed in the United States of America

Contents

Acknowledgments

Like Nephi, I was born of goodly parents who loved and lived the gospel as well as any parents could. Both my father and my mother instilled in me a love for the scriptures. I am thankful to them for providing me with opportunities for an education. It is to my father that I express my love and gratitude for reading *Voice from the Dust* (a narrative form of the Book of Mormon) to his children. I remember sitting on his lap as a child and seeing that big book in his hands and hearing stories of the faith of Book of Mormon prophets and leaders. I am confident that those moments were the beginnings of my love for and testimony of the Book of Mormon. It is to my mother that I express my heartfelt appreciation for a love for books and good literature.

I began forming ideas for this book while serving as a full-time missionary in the Spanish American Mission from 1961 to 1963. Following the mission I began my profession as a seminary teacher, and it was in the classroom that I gained experience in using the principles, practices, and skills presented in these pages. But it was while I served as mission president in the Cali Colombia Mission that I organized the material into a form that eventually resulted in this book.

I am thankful for the encouragement of colleagues in the Church Educational System and in the Missionary and Curriculum Departments of The Church of Jesus Christ of Latter-day Saints. In particular I thank David Christensen, Jerry Lund, Cory Bangerter, and George Horton. I am indebted to my good friend and editor Daniel Hogan, who offered many helpful suggestions.

The catalysts that propelled me to prepare a final manuscript and publish this book were my wife, Lonnie, and our six children. To Lonnie, Nathan, Laura, Andrea, Jason, Jared, and Jacob, I express my love and gratitude for your patience, support, and encouragement. If this publication helps you love the scriptures, live the truths in them, and follow the Savior more completely, the many hours I have devoted to the book's preparation will have been well spent.

Preface

This book is about the whys and "how to's" of studying and marking the scriptures. As used here, the word *scriptures* refers to the four standard works and also the words of the living prophets and Apostles whose messages are published in the official Church publications—the Conference Report, the *Ensign* and other Church magazines, and approved Church manuals.

I love these scriptures. I love the leaders—men and women—who have spoken and taught them. My emphasis in this work is exclusively on the four standard works—the Holy Bible, the Book of Mormon, the Doctrine and Covenants, and the Pearl of Great Price. However, I believe that what I have written here applies to all scriptures.

Sometime during my service as a young missionary in the Spanish American Mission (1961–63), I made a decision never to let a day go by without reading and studying the scriptures. I have kept that commitment. Few decisions have had a greater impact for good on my life than that one single resolve.

I must admit that the amount of time I have spent and the intensity with which I have studied has not been the same each day. There were days when five or ten minutes were all I gave, but on others I devoted an hour or more. The accumulation of those minutes and hours over the more than thirty years since has produced great dividends. As President Kimball stated concerning the accumulation of oil for the lamps of the ten virgins (see Matthew 25), drop by drop, day after day, a great reserve can be accumulated (see *Faith Precedes the Miracle*, pp. 253–56).

The accumulation of what I have gained is sacred to me. It has changed my life—spiritually, socially, temporally, and intellectually. Much of what I have learned is marked and annotated in the pages of my four standard works. Hundreds of lessons and thousands of ideas are found within those pages—organized, marked, cross-referenced, annotated, and orchestrated to be recalled at an instant.

As I studied, three patterns continued to emerge—the what, the how, and the why of scripture study. The first pattern, the what, consisted of those truths, doctrines, principles, and commandments that became clearer to me and are now eternally mine. I was learning and understanding the gospel. I was acquiring light and truth (see D&C 93:28).

The second pattern had to do with how I identified these truths and marked them for future use. I discovered that I used over and over certain scripture study techniques and methods. As I identified these techniques and gave each a name, it became easier to apply them in other chapters and verses (see chapters 4–12). It also became evident to me that great Church teachers and leaders I have known used those techniques over and over, although they never drew attention to how they had found such precious gems in the scriptures. Their focus was always on the what—the doctrines and principles found in the scriptures.

A major discovery for me was that scripture marking was related to the how of my scripture study. This discovery was stimulated by the questions students and missionaries asked me: "Brother Jensen, how do you mark your scriptures?" My discovery was as follows: As a general rule, scripture marking is a reflection of how you study the scriptures. Consequently, if you examine how you read and study the scriptures, you will generally find that marking them is an outgrowth of your study habits (see chapter 4).

When I started this book I proposed to focus on two themes: one, the scripture study techniques and methods I have found helpful to make the scriptures come alive—the how to's; and two, demonstrations of how to mark scriptures. However, as I immersed myself in those two themes I kept bumping into a third: why read, study, search, liken, and ponder the scriptures.

Someone has said that he who understands the "why" can live

with almost any "how." In fact there is a tendency to rebel when we do not know the "why." For example, when children are told by their parents to do something they often ask why. Wise parents take time to teach them the whys. Those who do not will often encounter resistance, rebellion, or blind obedience. Knowing the why is part of a divine pattern.

After Adam and Eve were cast out of the Garden of Eden they were taught the plan of redemption. "God gave unto them commandments, *after* having made known unto them the plan" (Alma 12:32; emphasis added). The plan of redemption (see Alma 12:32–33), the great plan of the Eternal God (Alma 34:9), the great plan of happiness (Alma 42:8) as it is called in the scriptures, is the grand why. It is the all-important reason for all that we do. Commandments, covenants, ordinances, and laws are the why and the how of God's plan for us.

The why and the how are both essential; therefore I have taken the time at the beginning of this book, following the divine pattern explained in the first part of Alma 12:32, to give what I have found to be the whys of scriptures study (see chapters 1, 2, and 3).

Finally, it is important to remember that the scripture study and marking techniques in this book are not an end in themselves; rather, they are the means to a far greater end. That desired end is that what is taught here will contribute to the Father's work and glory "to bring to pass the immortality and eternal life of man" (Moses 1:39). Furthermore, my prayer is that it will support the mission of The Church of Jesus Christ of Latter-day Saints, which is to invite all to come unto Christ and be perfected in Him (see D&C 20:59 and Moroni 10:32).

This book is not an official publication of The Church of Jesus Christ of Latter-day Saints. I alone am responsible for the views it expresses.

1

The Spirit and the Scriptures

Before developing specific suggestions for studying, searching, and marking the scriptures, it is essential to review principles related to our spirit nature and the spiritual preparation needed to study and search the scriptures.

Our Spirit Nature

Each of us is a dual being—an immortal spirit dwelling in a mortal body. We were born as spirit children to God our Heavenly Father. We lived with Him in our premortal state. President Brigham Young taught: "You are well acquainted with God our Heavenly Father. . . . You . . . lived in his house and dwelt with him year after year; and yet you are seeking to become acquainted with him, when the fact is, you have merely forgotten what you did know. [You] lived there . . . for ages." (*Discourses of Brigham Young*, p. 50.) In his presence we, along "with many others, received [our] first lessons in the world of spirits" (D&C 138:56). President Joseph F. Smith said:

> All those salient truths which come home so forcibly to the head and heart seem but the awakening of the memories of the spirit. Can we know anything here that we did not know before we came? . . .
> . . . If Christ knew beforehand, so did we. But in coming here, we forgot all, that our agency might be free indeed, to choose good or evil, that we might merit the reward of our own choice and conduct. But by the power of the Spirit, in the redemption of Christ, through obedience, we often catch a spark from the awakened

memories of the immortal soul, which lights up our whole being as with the glory of our former home. (*Gospel Doctrine*, pp. 13–14.)

It has been an interesting exercise for me to list some of those lessons that I learned in the premortal life. Among the many lessons learned would have been "the great plan of the Eternal God" (Alma 34:9), which included the Creation, the Fall, and the Atonement—the heart of the Father's plan. Other lessons included certainly would have been agency, obedience, eternal families, ordinances, and covenants. President J. Reuben Clark suggested that as spirits we may have learned how to govern a mortal body (see *Man, God's Greatest Miracle*, pp. 30–32).

My spirit knows much more than my mortal mind does. Gospel learning, then, may well be simply an awakening of those spirit memories. Hence the great need as parents and teachers to limit our teachings to the fundamental principles of the gospel, to those truths that the spirit knows and will readily recognize. Such fundamental truths are found in the scriptures—the four standard works and the words of the latter-day prophets and Apostles and others who speak by the Spirit (see D&C 68:1–4).

Our spirit nature was expressed by the Prophet Joseph Smith as follows: "All things whatsoever God in his infinite wisdom has seen fit and proper to reveal to us, while we are dwelling in mortality, in regard to our mortal bodies, are revealed to us in the abstract, and independent of affinity of this mortal tabernacle, but are revealed to our spirits precisely as though we had no bodies at all; and those revelations which will save our spirits will save our bodies." (*Teachings of the Prophet Joseph Smith*, p. 355.) Although the Prophet may not have said so, the corollary is that when the adversary chooses to send us a revelation he sends it directly to our mortal bodies. Those revelations that will enslave our bodies will also enslave our spirits. Thus the great challenge of mortality is the struggle between the spirit and the flesh.

For example, a family who strives to study the scriptures as a family every morning before school and work encounters the reality of this struggle. At the appointed hour, perhaps at 6:00 A.M., parents begin to awaken their children, saying "It's time for scripture reading." Not infrequently, some children have a sudden attack of a disease I have humorously called "mattress-itis." The child has a hard time detaching himself or herself from the warmth, comfort, and coziness of the pillow, the sheets and blankets, and the soft and comfortable mattress. This is a classic example of the conflict between the spirit and the flesh. The spirit desires and is hungry for the words of eternal life; however, the flesh is enveloped in the warmth and comfort of the bed.

The Spirit and the Word

There is no substitute for the Spirit of the Lord as you study and search the scriptures. In the first paragraph of the title page to the Book of Mormon, Moroni said that book had been "written by way of commandment, and also by the spirit of prophecy and of revelation." Inasmuch as it was written by the spirit of prophecy and of revelation, it should be read and studied as it was written—by the Spirit.

In a revelation to Joseph Smith, Oliver Cowdery, and David Whitmer, the Lord taught: "These words are not of men nor of man, but of me; wherefore, you shall testify they are of me and not of man; for it is my voice which speaketh them unto you; for they are given by my Spirit unto you" (D&C 18:34–35). In a later revelation the Lord taught that "my voice is Spirit" (D&C 88:66). If you substitute the word *Spirit* for the word *voice* in Doctrine and Covenants 18:35, it will read "For it is my *Spirit* which speaketh them unto you."

Few passages teach the spirit nature of the scriptures with greater clarity than this one: "For the word of the Lord is truth, and whatsoever is truth is light, and whatsoever is light is Spirit, even the Spirit of Jesus Christ. And the Spirit giveth light." (D&C 84:45–46.) Furthermore, Jesus taught His disciples that

Scripture Equations

Word = Truth
Truth = Light
Light = Spirit

Therefore the word is light and the word is Spirit.

"the words that I speak unto
 you, they are spirit" (John
 6:63).

Elder John A. Widtsoe taught a profound truth concerning the endowment in a statement I have adapted to the scriptures. "The [scriptures], which [have been] given by revelation can best be understood by revelation, and to those who seek most vigorously, with pure hearts, will the revelation be greatest" (*Temple Media Kit, Teacher's Guide,* p. 9).

That the words of the Lord are Spirit and can best be understood by the Spirit was impressed upon me one day as I was on an airplane that was preparing for takeoff. I retrieved a magazine from the pocket in the seat in front of me and thumbed through it, reading a few articles that caught my interest. Once the airplane was in the air, I returned the magazine to its pocket; I took from my briefcase my triple combination and placed it open on the tray table in front of me. I did not have a particular topic I was studying at the time, and I thumbed through a few pages, reading a few verses that caught my interest. Then the reality of what I had done struck me: "Jay, you have treated the scriptures like a common magazine, much like the one you just put away."

Whether at home or at work, traveling or sitting in meetings, how many times in my life have I taken the scriptures in my hands, treating them as if they were the daily newspaper, an ordinary book, a novel, or a magazine? I shudder to think of the number of times. Although I am not perfect in the practice, since that day on the airplane I have made a more conscious effort to treat the scriptures with the reverence and respect they deserve.

While we reverence these sacred books, we do not worship them. We worship the Father and the Son. By respecting the books and the words in them we show our reverence and respect for Deity.

One specific way in which I have reverenced them is to pray prior to studying and to express gratitude for the scriptures and ask for help in understanding them. Elder Howard W. Hunter said: "There is nothing more helpful than prayer to open our understanding of the scriptures. Through prayer we can attune our minds to see the answers to our searchings. . . . If we will ask, seek, and knock, the Holy Spirit will guide our understanding if we are ready and eager to receive." (*Ensign*, November 1979, p. 64.) I testify that increased light and truth come from the scriptures when I reverence and respect these books and the words in them, for they truly are the voice of the Lord to me, which is communicated through His Spirit to my spirit.

2

The Power of the Word

Prophets and missionaries in all dispensations have understood the power of the word of God. From the days of Adam "the Gospel began to be preached from the beginning, being declared by holy angels sent forth from the presence of God, and by his own *voice*, and by the gift of the Holy Ghost" (Moses 5:58; emphasis added). Preaching, declaring, and voices involve words. Words, written and spoken, are a means of communication. Not all words are of equal value. When it comes to the words of God, these take priority and precedence over all other words. There is power in His words.

I want to return to the great truth from the Doctrine and Covenants that was mentioned in the previous chapter: "For the word of the Lord is truth, and whatsoever is truth is light, and whatsoever is light is Spirit, even the Spirit of Jesus Christ" (D&C 84:45). To this is added the truth that "my voice is Spirit; my Spirit is truth" (D&C 88:66). The word of the Lord is His voice, and these words and His voice are Spirit. Furthermore, "the word of my power . . . is the power of my Spirit" (D&C 29:30). The promise to the faithful is that if we obtain His words and if we desire it we "shall have [His] Spirit and [His] word, yea, the power of God unto the convincing of men" (D&C 11:21). There is power in the word of God.

President Ezra Taft Benson will be remembered for wonderful teachings and counsel. Perhaps foremost among them is his emphasis on the Book of Mormon. It is exactly what Joseph Smith said of it: "I told the brethren that the Book of Mormon was the most correct of any book on earth, and the keystone of

6

6

our religion, and a man would get nearer to God by abiding by its precepts, than by any other book" (*Teachings of the Prophet Joseph Smith*, p. 194). Concerning the correctness and power of this keystone book, President Benson identified three reasons for reading and studying it: (1) it is the keystone of our religion in three ways—of our witness of Christ, of our doctrine, and of our testimony; (2) it was written for our day; and (3) it helps us draw nearer to God. (See *Ensign*, November 1986, pp. 4–7.) The Book of Mormon is true. It is of God. The Bible, the Doctrine and Covenants, and the Pearl of Great Price also contain the truth. They are inspired words of God.

The Book of Mormon contains a story line that is not found in the other scriptures. It has to do with the great challenge that missionaries and prophets faced in seeking to prepare a people for the first coming of the Lord (see Alma and Helaman and the first seven chapters of 3 Nephi).

If we liken the Book of Mormon to us in our day we can learn from what those missionaries and prophets did. This great volume of scripture can be looked at as a manual to help us prepare a people for the second coming of Christ. What worked well for the Book of Mormon leaders and missionaries was to preach the word. What prompted their actions might be summarized in one statement: They knew that there is power in the word of God.

Weaving its way through the Book of Mormon like a silver thread is a focus on that power. It begins with Nephi and ends with Moroni. The great ones in the books of Alma and Helaman, because they knew of the power of the word and knew that the first coming of Christ was not many years hence, set about to prepare a people to receive Him. Their principal method to prepare the people was simply to preach the word of God to them.

The account beginning in Alma chapter 4 shows the Church being threatened from within with pride, wealth, and inequality. Scorn and persecution followed, even to the point that "the Church began to fail in its progress" (Alma 4:10; see also Helaman 4:23; 3 Nephi 6:14). Alma saw the solution in the power of the word. He gave up the office of chief judge and devoted himself to the ministry so that "he might preach the word of God unto them, to stir them up in remembrance of their duty, and that

he might pull down, by the word of God, all the pride and craftiness and all the contentions which were among his people" (Alma
4:19). Preaching the word will lead people to do their duty.
Preaching the word will pull down pride, craftiness, and contentions. There is power in the word of the Lord.

During their fourteen-year missions (see Alma 17–26), the sons
of Mosiah "had much success in bringing many to the knowledge
of the truth; yea, by the power of their words many were brought"
to the gospel, the covenants and ordinances and the Church (Alma
17:4; see also Alma 19:31; 21:15–17; 22:12–14; 23:4; 26:13).

The power of the word of God is illustrated with a height,
breadth, and depth in Alma 31–34 that I have not found in other
scriptures.

Alma and other missionaries were aware of the apostate
Zoramites, whose rebellion and apostasy caused Alma's heart "to
sicken because of the iniquity of the people" (Alma 31:1). The
strategy to reclaim them, which is the theme and the central
thrust in reclaiming all wayward souls throughout the Book of
Mormon, was a faith and trust in the power of the word. The key
principles highlighted and marked in my scriptures are:

1. Preaching the word tended to lead people to do what was
   just. "And now, as the preaching of the word had a great
   tendency to lead the people to do that which was just—
   yea, it had had more powerful effect upon the minds of the
   people than the sword, or anything else, which had happened unto them—therefore, Alma thought it was expedient that they should try the virtue of the word of God"
   (Alma 31:5).
2. It (the preaching of the word) had had a more powerful
   effect than the sword or any other means.
3. In light of points 1 and 2 above, Alma chose to try or trust
   the virtue (power) of the word.

Alma 32 and the Power of the Word

Armed with the power of the word, Alma and his missionary
companions embarked on their missions to the Zoramites—to

preach the word in the synagogues, houses, and streets (see Alma 32:1). Not having much success among the prideful, affluent, apostate Zoramites, Alma and Amulek directed their efforts to the poor who, because of their afflictions, had humbled themselves. Being penitent and lowly in heart, "they were in a preparation to hear the word" (see Alma 32:6–8). We should note that these same three conditons of readiness—humbled, truly penitent, lowly in heart—must exist in our hearts if we are to experience the power of the word of God.

Perceiving these conditions, Alma invited the people to conduct an experiment upon his words, beginning with the first step of believing on the Lord's word (see Alma 32:22, 27).

To illustrate, he compared the word to a seed. Note that the seed in this chapter is not faith. Nowhere in the Book of Mormon is a seed compared to faith. That comparison is made in the New Testament (see Matthew 17:20 and Luke 17:6). While seeing Alma's words as comparing faith to a seed in Alma 32 may inspire a reader, to do so is to miss the substance and emphasis of the chapter. For his part, Alma clearly showed the word as the seed—the seed that must be nurtured by faith. (The key words in Alma 32 and the frequency of their appearance are as follows: *word(s)*=19; *know, knoweth, knowledge*=22; *faith*=17; *belief*=11. Words nurtured by faith lead to knowledge.)

To emphasize the significance of the experiment and that it is an experiment on the word, except for the first time the word *seed* is used in verse 28 substitute the word *word* each time the word *seed* appears, including pronouns used for *seed*. To illustrate, my scriptures are marked as follows:

> Now, we will compare the word unto a seed. Now, if ye give place, that a [word] may be planted in your heart, behold, if it be a true [word] or a good [word], if ye do not cast [the word] out by your unbelief, that ye will resist the Spirit of the Lord, behold, [the word] will begin to swell within your breasts; and when you feel these swelling motions, ye will begin to say within yourselves—It must needs be that this is a good [word], or that the word is good, for [the word] beginneth to enlarge my soul; yea, [the word] beginneth to enlighten my understanding, yea, [the word] beginneth to be delicious to me (Alma 32:28).

When the word of the Lord, which is light and truth and Spirit, is planted in my heart, it is easy to identify what happens inside me as indicated in one or a combination of three ways:

1. The word enlarges my soul.
2. The word enlightens my understanding.
3. The word begins to be delicious to me (see Alma 32:28).

Enlarge my soul. Words can have an impact inside us, sometimes so powerfully that we have a difficult time in expressing our thoughts and feelings. Perhaps when you hear the words of the Lord a strong feeling of love wells up within you. You want to be good or do good. Something powerful within you simply seeks a useful, beneficent expression. You can hardly contain yourself. Joy, love, peace, happiness, edification, rejoicing, humility, and meekness are but a few of the feelings you experience (see the fruits of the Spirit listed in Galatians 5:22–23).

Enlighten my understanding. Upon gaining a new insight or discovering a truth in the scriptures, have you ever said, either verbally or in your mind, "Ohhhh," or perhaps "Ah hah!" or "That makes sense," or "I have always believed that"? These thoughts or expressions are an illustration of having your understanding enlightened; the "light turns on" concerning something you read or heard. The seeds of truth are communicated spiritually. Pure intelligence or light and truth are communicated by the Spirit of the Lord to your spirit just as Joseph Smith said, precisely as though you had no mortal body at all (see *Teachings of the Prophet Joseph Smith,* p. 355).

Such had been the case with the wife of a mission president. As a teenager investigating the Church, she listened as the sister missionaries taught her the doctrine of the Godhead—three distinct personages. She explained: "Sisters, I have always believed that." Her church's theology supported the trinitarian concept of three in one, but she knew differently by the Spirit.

To be delicious. Often at the conclusion of a wonderful, spiritual missionary discussion where, as some missionaries put it, "the spirit was so thick you could cut it with a knife," the investigators may say something like this: "When will you come again?" Or, "I can hardly wait for the next discussion." These expressions illustrate the power of the word that was planted in their hearts. They simply are hungry for more of such delicious words. They feel something like Enos, who said, "And my soul hungered" (Enos 1:4). They feasted upon the word (see 2 Nephi 9:51; 31:20; 32:3).

To my mind, one of the greatest illustrations of these three truths is recorded in the testimony of Joseph Smith as he related the impact that James 1:5 had upon him. "Never did any passage of scripture come with more power to the heart [enlightened and enlarged] of man than this did at this time to mine. It seemed to enter with great force into every feeling of my heart [soul enlarged]. I reflected on it again and again [enlightened and delicious], knowing that if any person needed wisdom from God, I did; for how to act I did not know, and unless I could get more wisdom than I then had, I would never know." (Joseph Smith—History 1:12.)

We continue on with Alma 32 and the power of the word that was compared to a seed. The words that are planted are nourished by your faith—and at the same time they strengthen your faith. With each truth learned you will complete a sentence like Alma's description near the end of verse 30. "And now, behold, will not this strengthen your faith? Yea, it will strengthen your faith: for ye will say *I know that . . .*" (emphasis added.) Begin your sentence with "I know that . . . ," followed by the truth learned, such as "I know that the Book of Mormon is true." "I know that Joseph Smith was a true prophet." "I know that God hears and answers prayer." Truths, true seeds, words of truth bring forth their own likeness (see Alma 32:31).

As you conduct the experiment and plant seeds (true words), you will find that they will grow and you will know that they are good (see Alma 32:33). As you fulfill the conditions of each experiment, you gain or grow in knowledge, but only in that particular experiment. "And now, behold, is your knowledge perfect? Yea, your knowledge is perfect in that thing." (Alma 32:34.) Alma repeated (verse 34) the same three signs found at the end of verse 28 that help you to recognize the light and truth—the word swells your soul, your understanding is enlightened, and your mind expands. All of that occurs because the word of the Lord is light and truth (see Alma 32:35; D&C 84:45). However, as is indicated in verses 35 and 36, you do not have perfect knowledge of all things.

And where does faith fit into all of this? "Neither must ye lay aside your faith, for ye have only exercised your faith to plant the seed that ye might try the experiment to know if the seed was good" (Alma 32:36).

As you continue studying Alma 32, substituting the word *word* each time the word *seed* or the word *tree* appear, this word will take root in you, leading to life eternal.

To connect Alma 32 and 33 it is necessary to return to the question the poor people asked Alma. They explained to him that they were not permitted to enter into the synagogues they had built. They asked Alma what they should do to worship (see Alma 32:2–3, 5). It was not until what is now the next chapter that Alma answered the question concerning worship (see Alma 33:2–11).

Alma 33 and the Power of the Word

Chapter 33 begins with three questions that summarize chapter 32: (1) whether the people should believe in one God, (2) how they should plant the seed or the word, and (3) in what manner they should begin to exercise faith (see verse 1). Before answering the three questions, Alma answered the question concerning worship (see Alma 33:3–11). As he concluded this answer, he used the phrase "because of thy Son" twice (verse 11). This phrase also appears in verses 13 and 16 and seems to serve as a springboard to answer the three questions in verse 1.

The answer to all three questions is Jesus Christ—believe in Him, plant His word and teachings in you, and exercise faith in Him. Beginning with the Son of God is best illustrated by starting with the last verse in chapter 33 and working backward to verse 13. Alma said, "And now, my brethren, I desire that ye shall plant this word in your hearts" (Alma 33:23). What is the antecedent for the words *this word*? The answer is in verse 22, beginning with the command "begin to believe in the Son of God," following which is a brief, excellent summary of the Atonement:

1. Believe that He will come to redeem His people.
2. Believe that He shall suffer and die to atone for their sins.
3. Believe that He shall rise again from the dead, which shall bring to pass the resurrection.
4. Believe that all men shall stand before Him, to be judged at the last judgment day, according to their works.

"And now, my brethren, I desire that ye shall plant this word in your hearts" (Alma 33:23).

In verses 18–21 you will find an excellent illustration of typology. Moses lifted up the brass serpent—a type of Christ—and all who had been bitten by fiery flying serpents had only to look at the *type* and they would be healed. Plant this word in your hearts!

Furthermore, from verses 13–18, Alma quoted Zenos as saying that it was "because of the Son" that judgments were turned away and mercy extended. Plant this word in your hearts!

Finally, Alma concluded his message, saying: "And now, my brethren, I desire that ye shall plant this word in your hearts, and as it beginneth to swell even so nourish it by your faith. And behold, it [this word, the Son of God] will become a tree, springing up in you unto everlasting life. And then may God grant unto you that your burdens may be light, through the joy of his Son. And even all this can ye do if ye will. Amen." (Alma 33:23.) There is power in the word, which is Jesus Christ, through whom all burdens can be lifted, leading us to joy in Him, all of which we can experience.

Alma 34 and the Power of the Word

Having listened carefully to his companion, Alma, Amulek immediately began to build on what Alma had taught, saying: "He [Alma] hath exhorted you . . . that ye would have so much faith as even to plant the word in your hearts" (Alma 34:4). What word? Jesus Christ!

To emphasize that the word is in Jesus Christ, Amulek asked a question that may be the question of questions, one of the most important questions in time and eternity, one that all must not only ask but answer as well. He asked "whether the word be in the Son of God, or whether there shall be no Christ" (Alma 34:5). Beginning with the great Council in Heaven and from there to the fall of Adam and Eve and throughout mortality, this has been the great focal point. Is Jesus Christ really the Son of God? Does He really have power to redeem us? Did He really resurrect? Does He really live today?

The adversary has done all in his power to discredit, undermine, and destroy all belief in Jesus Christ and God the Father. In the premortal council Lucifer began his diabolical attempt to undermine the Father's plan, which included Jesus Christ as the center of the plan (see Moses 4:1–4). The alterations in the Holy Bible, the uninspired councils such as those of Nicaea and Chalcedon, and the mass of confusion passed on in the Protestant Reformation are examples of how Satan has attempted to destroy man's belief in and understanding of the divinity of Jesus Christ and His perfect and infinite atonement.

Attempts are made today to discredit and undermine Latter-day Saints as they declare with love and power the divinity of the Son of God. Elder Alexander B. Morrison provides an insight that summarizes well the position of our testimony of Christ and God. "For all of our history, Latter-day Saint beliefs on the nature and character of God have been dismissed with contempt by other churches. Mormons, they say, are ignoramuses, know-nothings, whose views on God and our relationship to Him are not worthy of respect and are certainly not Christian. If to be Christian requires acceptance of the God of the creeds and councils, I agree; we don't qualify. But the real question is who is in error, the Latter-day Saints or other Christians? To us there is and can be no question; we reject the unknown and unknowable God of the philosophers but wet with our tears the feet of the loving Father who spoke to the prophet Joseph Smith." (*Visions of Zion*, p. 64.)

Amulek captured as significant a question as I have found anywhere in the four standard works. I marvel at the inspiration in placing it as part of the great discourse on the power of the word started by Alma. Amulek added his teachings and testimony to those of Alma concerning the divine sonship of Jesus Christ. First, he referred to Alma's words (see Alma 34:6), which included references to the words of Zenos, Zenock, and Moses. Few verses in scripture contain more sublime and pure testimony than those of Amulek: "And now, behold, I will testify unto you of myself that these things are true. Behold, I say unto you, that I do know that Christ shall come among the children of men, to take upon him the transgressions of his people, and that he shall atone for the sins of the world; for the Lord God hath spoken it." (Alma 34:8.)

Following this pure testimony, he explained in beautiful detail the nature and power of the Atonement as part of "the great plan of the Eternal God" (Alma 34:9). The remainder of Alma 34 is a doctrinal explanation of the Atonement: how to exercise faith in Christ unto repentance; a plea to repent and prepare to meet God, which can only be done through the Atonement; and finally, among other things, an exhortation to deny no more the coming of Christ.

Nowhere in scripture have I found such a comprehensive treatise on the word as in Alma 31–34. When these chapters are viewed as a whole and with this focus, it is clear that the word is in Christ, and that when it is planted and nourished by faith, diligence, patience, and long-suffering, "it [the word] may take root in you, behold, by and by ye shall pluck the fruit thereof, which is most precious, which is sweet above all that is sweet, and which is white above all that is white, yea, and pure above all that is pure; and ye shall feast upon this fruit even until ye are filled, that ye hunger not, neither shall ye thirst." (Alma 32:42.) We should note that the old English use of the words *by and by* means "immediately" (see Bible Dictionary, "By and By," p. 627). While common usage today means just the opposite, the idea of immediately conforms to the promise that "if ye will repent and harden not your hearts, immediately shall the great plan of redemption be brought about unto you" (Alma 34:31; see also Mosiah 2:24).

Latter-day Prophets and Apostles and the Power of the Word

To receive revelation and knowledge concerning the revealed truths in the scriptures, as mentioned earlier, it is important to begin your daily scripture study time with prayer. As you study, frequently pray in your heart that you might be blessed with light and truth. After studying, it may be appropriate to conclude with prayer, thanking the Lord for the truths learned and seeking confirmation of them as well as power to live what you have learned.

To enjoy the power of the word, you should place a serious systematic study of the scriptures high on your list of daily priorities. Elder Howard W. Hunter's statement is representative of the counsel from Church leaders admonishing the Saints to set aside daily study time.

> Many find that the best time to study is in the morning after a night's rest has cleared the mind of the many cares that interrupt thought. Others prefer to study in the quiet hours after the work and worries of the day are over and brushed aside, thus ending the day with a peace and tranquility that comes by communication with the scriptures.
>
> Perhaps what is more important than the hour of the day is that a regular time be set aside for study. It would be ideal if an hour could be spent each day; but if that much cannot be had, a half hour on a regular basis would result in substantial accomplishment. A quarter of an hour is little time, but it is surprising how much enlightenment and knowledge can be acquired in a subject so meaningful. The important thing is to allow nothing else to ever interfere with our study. (*Ensign*, November 1979, p. 64.)

Whether you simply read for a set amount of time or a certain number of pages (quantity) or you systematically search and study (quality) depends on you and the goals you have set for yourself. You can, however, do both—quantity and quality.

President Benson reminded us of the importance of *daily* study: "I urge you to recommit yourselves to a study of the scriptures. Immerse yourselves in them daily so you will have the power of the Spirit." (*Ensign*, May 1986, p. 82.) President Benson reminded us often that it is the Spirit that matters most in this work (see Seminar for New Mission Presidents, June 1985, as cited in the *Missionary Guide*, p. 11). He quoted Elder Bruce R. McConkie that "men will be denied the sweet whisperings of the Spirit that might have been theirs unless they pay the price of studying, pondering, and praying about the scriptures" (as quoted in *Ensign*, May 1986, p. 81).

As you systematically study, have faith in the Lord and His

scriptures. You can understand what is written there. Scripture commentaries may help, but nothing can replace the standard works themselves. To understand what is in the scriptures, follow the counsel of Nephi: "Have ye inquired of the Lord?" (1 Nephi 15:8.) Alma accepted and followed that counsel: "I have inquired diligently of God that I might know—that is concerning the resurrection" (Alma 40:3). He then taught his son what he had learned (see Alma 40).

I have followed Nephi's counsel and Alma's example. One particular experience stands out. Prior to leaving for an assignment to Asia, I had recently read Alma's counsel to inquire diligently. I desired to experience what Alma experienced, not concerning the resurrection but to know and understand a gospel principle as to which I felt weak in my understanding. I believed with all my heart that I could learn as Alma had. During that entire assignment, night and morning and moments in between, I pleaded with the Lord to teach me concerning that particular doctrine. In airports, on airplanes, in hotels, and during other spare moments I studied and searched the scriptures. As a result, doors of revelation were opened to me. Day after day, understanding and insights came. I hold that trip sacred in my mind today because of what I acquired.

Few scriptural concepts are repeated more frequently than the following: "And I say unto you, Ask, and it shall be given you; seek, and ye shall find; knock, and it shall be opened unto you" (Luke 11:9). "If thou shalt ask, thou shalt receive revelation upon revelation, knowledge upon knowledge, that thou mayest know the mysteries and peaceable things—that which bringeth joy, that which bringeth life eternal" (D&C 42:61).

Few statements have had a greater impact on me to keep me in the scriptures than the following counsel from President Marion G. Romney:

> I don't know much about the Gospel other than what I've learned from the Standard Works. When I drink from a spring I like to get the water where it comes out of the ground, not down the stream after the cattle have waded in it. I appreciate other people's interpretation but when it comes to the Gosepl we ought to be

acquainted with what the Lord says and we ought to read it. You ought to read the Gospel, you ought to read the Book of Mormon and the Doctrine and Covenants and you ought to read all the scriptures with the idea of finding out what's in them and what the meaning is—not prove some idea of your own. Just read them and plead with the Lord to let you understand what he had in mind when he wrote them. (A talk to Seminary and Institute Coordinators, 3 April 1973.)

Elder Bruce R. McConkie taught that people who study the scriptures gain a dimension that cannot be achieved in any other way: "There's an increase in faith and a desire to do what's right and a feeling of inspiration and understanding that comes to people who study the gospel—meaning particularly the standard works—and who ponder the principles that can't come in any other way" (*Church News,* 24 January 1976, p. 4).

Thank God for the scriptures, especially the four standard works. In them is truly great power. In them you hear the voice of the Lord.

Consequences of Ignoring the Power of the Word

I had not thought to include a "wo" about scripture study, because everything I have learned and applied concerning the scriptures is inspiring, uplifting, strengthening, and fulfilling. From the scriptures we receive light and truth, and by them we are edified and rejoice together (see D&C 50:13–25). The humble followers of Christ enjoy the power of the word. It is simply positive. However, the scriptures themselves pronounce a "wo" upon those who fail to love and cherish these holy words.

The prophet Alma was very candid when he said: "If we have hardened our hearts against the word, insomuch that it has not been found in us, then will our state be awful, for then we shall be condemned" (Alma 12:13).

When the prophet Lehi and his family and others were in the desert, through revelation and inspiration the Lord provided constant direction. One of the means by which some of the direction came was through a ball. Lehi and his followers simply called it the ball. Later in the Book of Mormon we learn that it was called the Liahona, which according to language experts means "to Jehovah is light" or "of Jehovah is light" (see Reynolds and Sjodahl, *Commentary on the Book of Mormon*, 4:178–79). The Liahona worked "according to the faith and diligence and heed which we did give unto them [the pointers in the ball]" (1 Nephi 16:28).

In speaking to his son Helaman, Alma taught that the Liahona was a type. "And now I say, is there not a type in this thing? For just as surely as this director did bring our fathers, by following its course, to the promised land, shall the words of Christ, if we follow their course, carry us beyond this vale of sorrow into a far better land of promise." (Alma 37:45.)

What if His words are not found in us? What if we do not follow their course? In this same chapter (Alma 37:41–43), I have found five specific consequences for a lack of faith, diligence, and heed concerning the scriptures. Likening these five truths to us, it can be said of us and of them that–

1. Marvelous works ceased (v. 41).
2. They did not progress on their journey; they tarried in the wilderness (vv. 41–42).
3. They did not travel a direct course (v. 42).
4. They were afflicted (v. 42).
5. They did not prosper (v. 43).

For behold, it is as easy to give heed to the word of Christ, which will point to you a straight course to eternal bliss, as it was for our fathers to give heed to this compass, which would point unto them a straight course to the promised land (Alma 37:44).

A wonderful sermonette summarizing these truths appears early in the Book of Mormon, after the account of Nephi and his brothers' obtaining the plates of brass from Laban. Lehi and Nephi concluded that "it was wisdom in the Lord that we should carry them with us, as we journeyed in the wilderness towards the land of promise" (1 Nephi 5:22). We are not unlike Lehi and his family. We are in a great wilderness, surrounded by every sin, wickedness, and evil that perhaps has ever been assembled. It certainly is wisdom in the Lord that we should carry them—the scriptures—with us as we travel towards our land of promise, an inheritance in the kingdom of our Father. And it is not enough just to carry them in our hands. We must carry them in our hearts and in our minds.

3

The Three Ps of Scripture Study

The "Library of the Lord" (see Boyd K. Packer, *Ensign*, May 1990, pp. 36–38) has yet to reveal the height, the breadth, and the depth of light and truth hidden within its pages. To find more and more of these truths requires much effort on our part. The purpose of this chapter is to discuss and review what was introduced as part of a scripture study emphasis that was prepared a number of years ago in the Seminary and Institute program as part of the "Hold to the Rod" Scripture Motivation and Comprehension video series. These lessons were later incorporated into the Melchizedek Priesthood and the Relief Society personal study guides.

The "Hold to the Rod" series was designed to teach three basic principles—the promises of scripture study, the price to be paid to obtain fulfillment of the promises, and the processes or the methods for making the scriptures come alive. At the time this series was developed I was serving as the Director of Curriculum for the Seminaries and Institutes. I remember these three principles as the three Ps of scripture study. I am persuaded that all who follow the three Ps will achieve the desired outcomes of motivation and comprehension.

The Promises

Many are the promises to those who read, study, search, liken, and ponder these holy words. All these promises can be grouped into two categories—promises for the next life and promises for this life. An astonishing discovery to me was that most of the promises pertain to this life—to mortality. As you think about this profound truth, you can see the great love of God and His Son, who have given us their words to help us get through mortality successfully. Successfully graduating from mortality leads to the greatest promise of all—life eternal, which is the greatest gift of God (see D&C 14:7).

Promises for the next life. Promises for the next life consist of perfection, exaltation, and eternal life. Consider the following:

1. The scriptures were given that "the man of God may be perfect" (2 Timothy 3:17).
2. "They did press their way forward, continually holding fast to the rod of iron, until they came forth and fell down and partook of the fruit of the tree" (1 Nephi 8:30).
3. "Wherefore, if ye shall press forward, feasting upon the word of Christ, and endure to the end, behold, thus saith the Father: Ye shall have eternal life" (2 Nephi 31:20).
4. The word of God will lead the "man of Christ in a strait and narrow course . . . and land their souls . . . at the right hand of God in the kingdom of heaven" (Helaman 3:29–30).

Promises for this life. As mentioned above, the astounding discovery for me concerning the scriptures, the word of God, is that most of their promises pertain to mortality. Consider the following four general categories of promises—testimony, power, increase, and other.

Promise of a Testimony of Jesus Christ

No promise is more supernal than that of a knowledge and testimony of Jesus Christ. Consider these few references:

1. Search the scriptures, [and if you do, you will find that they] testify of me (John 5:39).[1]

---

1. I believe that this scripture is misused at times. Although it can be used as a general command or exhortation to search the scriptures, the specific context reveals that the Savior was chastising the Jews for not believing the witnesses of Him—John, the works of Jesus, and the Father Himself (see John 5:36–37). Jesus then said: "Search the scriptures; for in them ye think ye have eternal life; and they are they which testify of me" (John 5:39). The Jews erred in thinking that eternal life was to be found in the scriptures. If they searched them, they (like us) would find that they do testify of Jesus Christ, and He leads us to eternal life.

2. These things are written so you might believe that Jesus is the Christ, the Son of God (John 20:31).
3. The Book of Mormon is another testament of Jesus Christ and is to convince the Jew and Gentile that Jesus is the Christ, the Eternal God (Book of Mormon, title page).
4. The scriptures speak of Jesus Christ and persuade readers to believe in Him (2 Nephi 33:4).
5. The things written on the plates of gold and those of brass brought people to the knowledge of the Lord their God and to rejoice in Jesus Christ their Redeemer (Alma 37:8–9).

Promises of Power

1. Power to live righteously:
   - The word of the Lord is a lamp to my feet (Psalm 119:105).
   - The scriptures are profitable for correction and for instruction in righteousness (2 Timothy 3:16).
   - Preaching the word stirs people up in the remembrance of their duty (Alma 4:19).
   - Preaching the word led people to do what was just (Alma 31:5).
2. Power to overcome evil:
   - The word of the Lord can keep you from the paths of the destroyer (Psalm 17:4).
   - With the word of the Lord (law and commandments) you can refrain from evil ways (Psalm 119:98–101).
   - Through the precepts of the Lord you can hate every false way (Psalm 119:104).
   - The fiery darts of the adversary will not overpower those who hearken and hold fast to the word of God (1 Nephi 15:24).
   - Those who lay hold upon the word of God will have power to divide asunder the cunning, the snares, and the wiles of the devil (Helaman 3:29).
   - Whoso treasures up the Lord's words will not be deceived (Joseph Smith—Matthew 1:37).

3. Power to convince:
    *   The scriptures are profitable for reproof (2 Timothy 3:15–17).
    *   Having searched the scriptures and knowing the word of God, Alma and the sons of Mosiah taught with the power and authority of God (Alma 17:2–3).
    *   The preaching of the word had a more powerful effect upon the minds of the people than the sword or anything else (Alma 31:5).
    *   These things (scriptures on the plates of gold and those of brass) convinced many of the error of their ways (Alma 37:8–9).
    *   If you first seek to obtain the Lord's word, your tongue shall be loosed (D&C 11:21).
    *   If one has the desire, the Spirit and the word lead to the power of God unto the convincing of men (D&C 11:21).
    *   When you treasure up in your mind continually the words of life, it shall be given you in the very hour what to give to every man (D&C 84:85).
4. Power to call down the powers of heaven:
    *   As we   search the words of the prophets our faith becomes unshaken, till we can command in the name of Jesus (Jacob 4:6).
    *   Those who believe the prophecies (the scriptures) become firm and steadfast in the faith (Helaman 15:7–8).
5. Power to change minds and hearts:
    *   The word of the Lord combined with the Spirit wrought a mighty change in the hearts of King Benjamin's people (Mosiah 5:1–3).
    *   Through Abinadi's words there came a mighty change in Alma's heart (Alma 5:11– 12).
    *   Alma preached the word and a mighty change was wrought in his hearers' hearts (Alma 5:13).
    *   The preaching of the word had a more powerful effect upon their minds than the sword or anything else (Alma 31:5).

• The prophecies which were written led Lamanites to faith in Christ and to repentance, which led to a change of heart (Helaman 15:7–8).

Promises of Increase

1. Increase of knowledge and understanding:
   • Through the Lord's precepts, understanding comes (Psalm 119:104).
   • What was written earlier was written for our learning (Romans 15:4).
   • The holy scriptures are profitable for doctrine (2 Timothy 3:16).
   • The holy scriptures are able to make us wise (2 Timothy 3:15).
   • The words of Christ will tell us all things that we should do (2 Nephi 32:3).
   • He that will not harden his heart, to him is given the greater portion of the word (Alma 12:10).
   • The holy scriptures are given of the Lord for our instruction (D&C 33:16).
2. Increase in testimony:
   • The law of the Lord converts the soul (Psalm 19:7).
   • The word (seed) planted and nourished will lead us to know (Alma 32:30, 34–35).
   • The things written on the plates brought many Lamanites to a knowledge of the Lord their God (Alma 37:8–9).
   • When you have the Lord's word, you may of a surety know His doctrine (D&C 11:16).
3. Increase in spirituality:
   • Nephi's soul delighted in the scriptures and his heart pondered them (2 Nephi 4:15).
   • Souls were illuminated by the light of the everlasting word (Alma 5:7).
   • First seek to obtain the Lord's word and you shall have His Spirit (D&C 11:21).

4. Increase in love, happiness, hope, and joy:
    - Through the patience and comfort of the scriptures we may obtain hope (Romans 15:4).
    - The rod of iron led to the love of God (1 Nephi 11:25).
    - The pleasing word of God heals the wounded soul (Jacob 2:8).
    - Searching the scriptures leads to hope (Jacob 4:6).
    - It is to the sacred word of God that we owe all our happiness (Alma 44:5).
    - Listening to the Lord's words leads to peace (D&C 19:23).
5. Increase in discernment:
    - The word of God is a discerner of the thoughts and intents of the heart (Hebrews 4:12).
    - Whoso treasures up the Lord's words will not be deceived (Joseph Smith—Matthew 1:37).

Other Promises

1. If the Israelites would love and teach His word, their days and those of their children would be prolonged in the land (Deuteronomy 11:18–21).
2. By meditating upon and observing what was written the Israelites would make their way prosperous and would have good success (Joshua 1:8).
3. What was written on Nephi's plates would persuade his people to do good (2 Nephi 33:4; Ether 8:26).
4. The things written on the gold plates and the brass plates enlarged the memory of Alma's people (Alma 37:8).

The Price

While I was presiding over a mission of the Church in South America, Elder Gene R. Cook toured the mission and taught me a concept that has become a governing principle in my life: "When your priorities are out of order, you lose power." Making the statement positive, it reads "when your priorities are in order, you gain power." The many promises of power listed in this chapter should be sufficient to convince anyone to pay whatever price would be required to obtain all the Lord has promised.

A searching question to help me in my priorities concerning scripture study is "Why do I do what I do when I know what I know?" Knowing and doing are two different things. There are many in the Church who permit things of eternal importance to be at the mercy of things that are of a lesser importance.

Why do we not read the scriptures? The reasons vary, such as, "I don't have time," "The scriptures are hard to understand, especially the Bible," "I am too tired at night when I get home and I leave too early in the morning," and on and on. One of the greatest obstacles to scripture study is television. Watching something on television is often the path of least resistance.

Perhaps the most candid answer as to why we do not read the scriptures is what the Lord told the Prophet Joseph Smith: "Your minds in times past have been darkened because of unbelief, and because you have treated lightly the things which you have received—which vanity and unbelief have brought the whole church under condemnation" (D&C 84:54–55). Unbelief, pride, and vanity creep into our lives and we let them crowd out the scriptures. We cannot blame the scriptures, but only ourselves.

An example of the above is an experience I had that convinced me that those who really want to find a way do so. The others find an excuse and fail to exercise faith in the promises of the Lord; in other words, they exercise unbelief.

I was assigned to reorganize a stake presidency. In each interview for the calling of stake president I briefly inquired into the person's personal scripture study habits. True to form, a few offered excuses. One fine brother was truly an inspiration. He said that he took a bus to work each morning about 6:15 A.M. The trip usually took about one hour, so he arrived at about 7:10 or 7:15 A.M. Because he did not have to begin work until seven-thirty, he took advantage of those fifteen minutes each morning to read the Book of Mormon. Also, he said, sometimes he read it during his lunch break. The light of the gospel shined in his eyes as he told me this. He enjoyed the promises because his priorities were in order.

Those who say they do not have time often admit to watching television. The following illustrates how much you can study and read instead of watching television. "Holding the priesthood means being commissioned by the Lord to act as he would act if he were here personally. Is your television habit compatible with that holy commission? If you have a twenty-hour-a-week television habit and would repent and convert it into a gospel study habit, in one year you could read or reread the Book of Mormon, the Doctrine and Covenants, the Pearl of Great Price, and the entire Bible." (William R. Bradford, *Ensign*, November 1979, p. 37.)

Elder Bradford went on to say that during that same year you could also read about twelve volumes of Church books and the monthly Church periodicals. This is based on ten pages per hour, while an average reader reads 20 pages an hour. This approach still leaves you 10 hours a week for other Church and civic service. (See ibid., pp. 37–38.)

The price? For each of us it is different. You simply have to be like the man I interviewed. He exemplified principles I had learned from Elder Cook when he toured our mission and taught our missionaries principles of how to make covenants and how to exercise faith.

1. Prayerfully select or set a goal. Be sure you do not set a goal that would be against the Lord's will.
2. Write it down. Missionaries are always taught that a goal not written is only a wish, and, like smoke in the air, vanishes.
3. Make the goal very specific and doable. Define it.
4. Set a time to have it done. Be specific—write down the day of the week—even the hour, if possible—not next week or next month.
5. Share this commitment with someone you know and respect. They will help to hold you accountable.
6. To that individual and to the Lord, give an accounting of what you have done.
7. Expect tribulations. They will surely come. Remember that you receive no witness (or results) until after the trial of your faith (see Ether 12:6).
8. Double your efforts and faith in the face of the tribulation. One way that you double your faith is through righteous works.

9. Exercise faith in God, faith in Christ, faith in their promises, and faith in yourself and the gifts and talents they have given you to accomplish righteous purposes.

The Processes

The processes are the how to's of scripture study—the methods and techniques. The specific techniques will be treated in the chapters that follow, but some principles that apply to all techniques have helped me to use each of the "how-to's" with greater effectiveness.

The Lord has given specific commandments concerning what we are to do with the scriptures. For example, "thou shalt read this law before all Israel" (Deuteronomy 31:11), "study my word" (D&C 11:22), "search these commandments" (D&C 1:37), "ye ought to search the scriptures" (Alma 33:2), "ponder upon the things which I have said" (3 Nephi 17:3), and finally "liken them [the words of the prophets] unto yourselves" (1 Nephi 19:24). Read, study, search, ponder, and liken. (The words "read the scriptures," as a command, are not in the scriptures. It is more commonly found with "when ye read these things," or "I would ask if ye have read the scriptures" [Alma 33:14], or "I did read many things to them" [1 Nephi 19:22]. None of the 118 uses of the word *read* in the scriptures communicates an imperative such as we find in the use of *study* or *search*.)

Each verb communicates a different activity to be done with the scriptures. Each one is important and produces different results. Consider the following definitions or synonyms of each verb:

Read — Peruse, look over, investigate.

Study — Explore, investigate, research, review, survey.

Search — Examine, explore, inspect, investigate, scrutinize. The word *search* may imply an attempt to find something hidden.

Ponder — Meditate, contemplate, reflect upon, think about, weigh heavily. Pondering involves prayerful reflection and contemplation.

Liken — Compare. How is something similar or alike?

What does it parallel or resemble? Examples of likening from the scriptures are parables, allegories, similes, types, and symbols. Applying the scriptures to ourselves is a subset of likening.

Consider the following illustration of doing more than reading the scriptures.

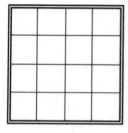

Count the squares.

At first glance you may say 16, or perhaps 17 when you identify the large one that encloses the 16. However, when you study and search, you will find there are exactly 30. This can be likened to the scriptures, in that there is more than meets the eye. In case you did not find all 30, here they are.

By dividing it into fourths you can see four more, making 21.

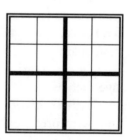

There is one square in the center of the box, making 22.

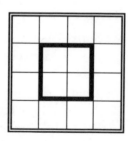

But there are still eight more. Four of them are found by starting at each corner and moving from left to right three boxes, down three, to the left three, and go up three to the corner you started with, as shown. Repeat this with each corner and you have four more.

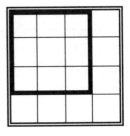

The final four are found by starting at the upper left corner. Go to the right one box, go down two, to the right two, go up two, and return to your starting point, as illustrated . Repeat the process on each side of the large box. With these four, we now have 30 squares.

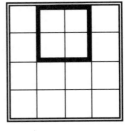

Few illustrations capture better the concept of what can be found in the scriptures. There is more than meets the eye. Often a friend or a teacher will point out something in the scriptures, such as a square that you did not see before; it had escaped your knowledge or understanding. Frequently, in the quiet moments of prayerful study, early in the morning or late at night, by the power of the Holy Spirit something jumps off the page with a clarity and an understanding not seen or felt before. It is as the Prophet Joseph Smith said, "pure intelligence"—a revelation by the power of the Spirit directly to your mind. It is as if the printer had played a trick on you and printed that verse or that truth in your scriptures since the last time you studied them.

Suddenly you begin to read the white space between the lines. Or you read beyond the lines. You see things only available to the pure in heart who humbly seek personal revelation. In fact, some students of the scriptures feel that instead of being a flat surface, the square suddenly becomes a cube, illustrating again that there is a height, breadth, and depth to the scriptures that we have yet to find.

Another illustration that has helped me is the following: Looking at the scriptures is like looking at a favorite tree, one half of which is above ground and has always been open to study and examination, either close up (micro) or from a distance (macro). But now you realize that one half of the tree is hidden beneath the ground—the roots. These life-giving extremities of a tree send nourishment to all that is visible above ground. What we can see of the tree above ground can be likened to reading and studying. Like the tree that can be examined close up or at a distance, the scriptures written in columns, verses, sentences, paragraphs, words, and so forth, can be examined either close up or at a distance. However, the roots under the ground are hidden to the mortal eye. It is so also with the scriptures: much is hidden to the mortal eye. Only by searching, pondering, likening, and prayerful reflection will we discover hidden truths.

Until we discover in the scriptures the full tree—roots, trunk, branches, and leaves—we have yet to find the promised height, breadth, and depth in those holy books. It is a truth that some of the most precious truths in the scriptures are hidden the deepest and with the greatest care. The Prophet Joseph Smith reminded us that "the things of God are of deep import; and time, and experience, and careful and ponderous and solemn thoughts can only find them out" (*Teachings of the Prophet Joseph Smith*, p. 137).

4

Scripture Marking

My students in Church Educational System classes, our missionaries, and members of the Church who attended my classes or the firesides where I spoke, often asked: "Brother Jensen, how do you mark scriptures?" My answer is reduced to one simple principle: *My scripture marking is a reflection of how I study scriptures.* Each verse that I have marked is simply a reflection of a particular scripture study technique. This means that the technique I use determines the appearance of the marking of a verse on the page.

Because this book is primarily a "how to study and mark the scriptures" book, I have chosen to discuss scripture marking at the beginning, knowing that throughout the chapters that follow you will find illustrations of marked verses. My answer to my students and missionaries—and to you the reader—is: Examine each verse I have included and you will see that each one illustrates one or more of the techniques. Therefore, the more important question in my mind is, How do you or should you study the scriptures? Once you have resolved that, let your study methods determine how you mark them. If you have not identified some simple study methods, perhaps this book will help you.

Some students of the scriptures have not thought through the question of why or how to mark them. Consequently, they may be among those who have indiscriminately marked them, not having given the idea much thought. Similarly, they may have seen someone else's marked books and adopted the model they saw. Indiscriminate marking or shading entire columns and chapters may be no better than leaving them unmarked. When you underline or shade everything, everything then stands out—entire columns and pages. When you return to those marked pages at some future date, you must search again to find what it was that impressed you in the first place.

Why Mark Scriptures?

Two important reasons for marking scriptures are (1) to facilitate recall, to retrieve truth from those sacred pages, and (2) to facilitate teaching and learning.

To facilitate recall. When you marked a verse, something impressed you and you wanted to be able to remember it or retrieve it in the future. The very reason why the scriptures are organized into books, chapters, and verses is to facilitate finding what is in them.

Scripture marking can be viewed as an organized filing system. Filing systems exist primarily for retrieving information. Many offices abound with filing cabinets—two, three, four, and sometimes five drawers in each. In each drawer are folders, usually neatly organized and tabbed to facilitate retrieving what has been filed.

Marking each of the four standard works of the Church might be viewed as organizing one of the drawers in a filing cabinet. When you open the book, every marked reference should be as easy to find for you as trying to locate a specific folder in a filing cabinet.

Unfortunately, some offices do not follow sound filing procedures. Their filing cabinets are poorly organized. Rather than a filing system, theirs would best be known as a "piling" system. Stacks of papers, folders, and documents are haphazardly placed in the files with little hope that anyone could easily retrieve some needed document.

I am reminded of an experience as a writer on a Church writing committee. One of the committee members was the brunt of all jokes when it came to a "piling" system. When you walked into his office, stacks of papers were found on his desk, to the side of his desk, on top of the filing cabinet, to the side of the filing cabinet, on shelves, and so forth.

I have seen some copies of the four standard works that remind me of my friend's piling system in his office. As I thumbed through them I saw page after page of indiscriminate underlining, shading, and other markings. We must assume that the markings made sense to the owner, as they should. But there is a better way.

The most common scripture marking I see is an entire verse, or verses, or chapters shaded, usually by a "hi-liter" in one solid color. Some I have seen have multi-color. As to effect, I have been unable to see a significant difference between shading everything and shading nothing. The only visual difference is the color on the page. The shading of an entire verse or column indicates that everything in it is important to the reader. My plea is for greater discrimination in scripture marking. Think through what you have found in the verse that is important to you and then make that idea, principle, or truth stand out so you can remember and use it.

Marked scriptures should help you to easily locate and retrieve valuable truths, doctrines, principles, and commandments. When scriptures are marked in an orderly, systematic way, you not only can retrieve what you want but can also present it to someone else.

To facilitate teaching and learning. Another reason for marking scriptures is to facilitate teaching and instruction. President David O. McKay taught: "There are three things which must guide all teachers: First, get into the subject; . . . second, get that subject into you; third, try to lead your pupils to get the subject into them—not pouring it into them, but leading them to see what you see, to know what you know, to feel what you feel" (*Gospel Ideals*, p. 424).

When your scriptures are marked to aid recall, it is likely they will also promote teaching and learning. They will facilitate what President McKay encouraged in leading others to see what you see in the scriptures, to know what you know from the scriptures, and to feel what you feel about the scriptures. Those I look up to and admire as students of the scriptures have their four standard works marked in such a way as to draw from those pages literally hundreds of lessons, lessons for their own benefit and comfort or to share with others.

When you have organized your scriptures to facilitate teaching and learning, you will find yourself teaching more directly *from* the scriptures. President Lee reminded us to teach from the scriptures: "All that we teach in this Church ought to be couched in the scriptures. It ought to be found in the scriptures. We ought to choose our text from the scriptures." (Harold B. Lee, *Improvement Era*, January 1969, p. 13.) Well-marked scriptures will help you to do just that.

How to Mark Scriptures

As stated above, your scripture marking system will normally be a reflection of how you read and study the scriptures. (Techniques to study the scriptures are in the chapters that follow.) However, in addition to this basic principle and the two principles concerning why we might want to mark scriptures, there are other principles about scripture marking that I have found useful.

1.   Simplicity. Scripture marking should be simple, not complex. Here I underlined the phrase "he was obedient unto the word" because it represents a simple truth. I underlined the word *wherefore* because it sets up a cause and effect relationship between being obedient and doing.

"And it came to pass that he was obedient unto the word of the Lord, wherefore he did as the Lord commanded him" (1 Nephi 2:3).

2.   Personalize it. Make scripture marking work for you. You are the one who will draw upon what you have marked. You will be the one who will find it and teach it. In the example at the right, I personalized the phrase "a beautiful process" and wrote it above the words "as he read" to remind me that as I

A beautiful process
"And it came to pass that as he read, he was filled with the Spirit of the Lord" (1 Nephi 1:12).

read scriptures I, too, will be filled with the Spirit.

3. Decide what color pencil or markers to use. Some use only one color such as a red pencil. Others use two colors, perhaps red and blue. Still others use a variety of colors. On a rare occasion, I remember, I saw some key doctrines marked according to a color—Godhead yellow, apostasy green, Restoration blue, Atonement red, and so forth. Personally I have never found the multicolor system useful, nor have I seen someone else's marked scriptures that used this system effectively. Frankly, there are more doctrines than there are useable colors. In the example, I underlined the word *atonement* because of the doctrine concerning the Atonement, and the phrase "the great plan of the Eternal God" because it is one of several titles given to the plan of salvation. The superscripts "a" and "b" are shaded to point me to the footnotes for additional references concerning the Atonement (footnote 9a) and the plan (footnote 9b).

4. Use high-liters cautiously. Some bleed through the page and make a real

"For it is expedient that an ªatonement should be made; for according to the great ᵇplan of the Eternal God there must be an atonement made or else all mankind must unavoidably perish; yea, all are hardened; yea, all are fallen and are lost; and must perish except it be through the atonement which it is expedient should be made" (Alma 34:9).

mess. Again I emphasize the
basic principle: <u>Your scripture
marking system is a reflection
of how you study the scriptures.</u> And of course the entire
emphasis of this book is to
illustrate how to study, search,
and ponder the scriptures.

Whether you shade a
word or a phrase or underline
it is up to you. My preference
is to underline using a red
pencil. (Because I feel so
strongly about the uselessness
of shading entire verses, the
question of enclosing them in
boxes or circling the numbers
of the verses is a moot issue.)
My annotations and marginal
comments are also written in
red, with an occasional note
in blue pencil for emphasis or
contrast.

5. Do not duplicate
cross-references. Footnotes on
each page are to help you
study and search the scriptures. Before annotating a
cross-reference, check first to
see if it is in a footnote. In this
illustration, the footnote 11a
has four excellent references
concerning this seer; therefore, I shade only the superscript "a" in the first line of
verse 11.

[a]"But a seer will I raise up
out of the fruit of thy loins;
and unto him will I give
power . . ." (2 Nephi 3:11).

6. Add to the footnotes. For lack of space, not all relevant cross-references could be included when the scriptures were prepared for publication. Add your own cross-references using available space in the margins, between columns, in the white space following the end of a sentence in a verse, and along with the other footnotes. Note here that I added five references where the word *merits* appears in the Book of Mormon, and I also included a definition of the word. Substituting synonyms for the word *merits* deepens my understanding of this aspect of the Atonement. Also, note that I have numbered these three words to form a list (see chapter 6).

7. Annotate. In the margins and other available space on a page, add written comments. I have included the following kinds of annotations: quotations from latter-day prophets that clarify or add meaning to a verse; definitions of words, especially archaic word meanings; personal impressions. In fact, with the passing of years, I find myself doing more annotating than underlining.

2 Nephi 31:19
Alma 24:10
Helaman 14:13
Moroni 6:4
D&C 3:20
Merits=Rewards, virtues, achievements "presence of God, save it be through the (1) merits, and (2) mercy, and (3) grace of the Holy Messiah, . . ." (2 Nephi 2:8).

"And the Lord said unto him: I give unto you power that ye shall baptize this people when I am again ascended into heaven" (3 Nephi 11:21). I have written the following note in the margin: "Baptism (or form of word) appears 13 times in vv. 21–41. Word doctrine appears 9 times."

8. Insert quotations and outlines. Longer quotations and outlines of topics and ideas that cannot be written in the available space in the margins can be typed on thin paper and glued in between the pages.

In summary, remember these two principles governing scripture marking: (1) scripture marking is normally a reflection of how you study scriptures; (2) mark scriptures to facilitate recall and teaching and learning.

5

Principles of Substitution

In the first four chapters we reviewed the Spirit and the scriptures, the power of the word, the three Ps of scripture study, and finally, marking scriptures. With this foundation in place we will now discuss techniques to study and search the scriptures. Generally the people I have talked with want to gain more out of their scripture study but often have not known how. These ideas I recommend have helped me, and I have taught them enough that I have discovered that many have used similar techniques although they may not have put the same "handle" or description to the technique. I have also discovered that there seems to be a receptivity for such techniques.

Some of the most valuable lessons we learn in life are from our children. One morning we were reading the Book of Mormon as a family. Our youngest daughter, about ten years old at the time, interrupted our reading with this startling comment: "Dad, this sure is boring." Rather than being preachy or defensive (something that I had done before) I was blessed to ask why. She simply said, "Dad, it is so confusing to me. I don't know who is talking. I don't know who they are talking to and sometimes I don't know what they are talking about." Her frustrations were, and are, not unlike those felt by many wonderful Saints.

These helpful techniques that I had taught for years to students in classrooms, missionaries in the field, and other members in firesides were good for them, but I had not applied them as I should have in our family scripture reading time. I vowed to repent and use them wisely with our own children, beginning with the simple technique of substitution.

Substituting Your Name in the Place of Scripture Names

Substitution is a technique that many students of the scriptures use. For some it is almost automatic to read or insert their
name or other names in the place of the person's name in the
verse. Yet for others this is a new idea. For example, many parents
of missionaries receive letters of gratitude from their missionary
sons and daughters, quoting the first verse from the Book of Mormon and substituting their name for Nephi's: "I, [Jay], having
been born of goodly parents, therefore [Jay] was taught somewhat in all the learning of my father [Ruel W. Jensen] . . . " (1
Nephi 1:1).

Another example: "And now it came to pass that when [Jay
Jensen] had received this epistle [or letter] his heart did take
courage, and was filled with exceedingly great joy because of the
faithfulness of [Nathan, Jason, Jared, Jacob—the names of our
sons who wrote to us while serving missions]" (Alma 62:1). Few
words in scripture better capture the feelings of a parent after
reading each letter from a missionary son or daughter, for these
letters are as important to the family as Paul's letters were to the
Corinthians.

Applying this technique can be a real call to repentance in
some instances. Doctrine and Covenants 30 records David Whitmer's being severely chastened for failure to serve diligently. Substituting my name for David's, the verses read as follows:

> Behold, I say unto you, [Jay], that [Jay has] feared man and
> [has] not relied on [the Lord] for strength as [Jay] ought.
> But [Jay's] mind has been on the things of the earth more than
> on the things of me, your Maker, and the ministry whereunto [Jay
> has] been called; and [Jay has] not given heed unto my Spirit, and to
> those who were set over [Jay], but has been persuaded by those
> whom [the Lord has] not commanded.
> Wherefore, [Jay is] left to inquire for [Jay's] self at [the Lord's]
> hand, and ponder upon the things which [Jay has] received. (D&C
> 30:1–3.)

Before you substitute your name or as you do so, often it is
helpful to include the names of the actual people in the context of

the verse. This is illustrated in a revelation given to Edward Partridge. "And I [the Lord] will lay my hand upon you [Edward Partridge] by the hand of my servant Sidney Rigdon, and you [Edward Partridge] shall receive my Spirit, the Holy Ghost, even the Comforter, which shall teach you [Edward Partridge] the peaceable things of the kingdom" (D&C 36:2).

After you have substituted the name referred to in this verse, you can easily remove that name and put yours in its place. By your substituting your name and the name of the individual who ordained you to your current priesthood office or set you apart to your current calling, this verse will take on greater personal meaning. For example, President Spencer W. Kimball ordained me a high priest. Substituting his name and my name, the verse reads as follows: "And I [the Lord] will lay my hand upon [Jay Jensen] by the hand of my servant [Spencer W. Kimball], and [Jay Jensen] shall receive my Spirit, the Holy Ghost, even the Comforter, which shall teach [Jay Jensen] the peaceable things of the kingdom."

How much more sacred to me my ordination is when I personalize the scriptures in this way! It is the Lord who ordains and sets apart. However, he does it *by the hands of* his earthly servants.

There are, of course, references where it is not appropriate to insert your name. You must use wisdom, good judgment, and good taste as you do so. For example, only the two counselors in the First Presidency may appropriately insert their names in Doctrine and Covenants 90:6, this verse being a revelation concerning the organization of the First Presidency.

May a woman insert her name where the Lord speaks to a man, or may a man insert his name where the Lord speaks to a woman? You will have to determine the appropriateness of doing so. There is an excellent illustration in which the Lord is speaking to Emma Smith (see D&C 25) where a woman may and probably should insert her name as an elect lady. I had not inserted my name in this important section until I discovered a phrase in the final verse. "This is my voice unto all" (D&C 25:16). Does the word *all* refer to all women or can it refer to all men as well? I believe it can refer to men also. For example, substitute your name in this verse and, if you are married, the name of your spouse. "Continue in the spirit of meekness, and beware of pride.

Let thy soul delight in thy husband [wife], and the glory which shall come upon him [her]." (D&C 25:14.)

Certainly all men and women should continue in the spirit of meekness and beware of pride. All men and women should delight in their spouses and the glory, light, and truth that come upon them.

Substituting Nouns for Pronouns

Have you ever noticed how often there are different speakers or hearers in a chapter of scripture? Have you ever stopped to notice the number and frequency of pronouns that are used in a typical chapter of scriptures? Nouns and pronouns and scripture study—do you remember your high school English classes? A pronoun is a word that replaces a noun. They abound in the scriptures—I, we, ye, thee, thou, thine, my, ours, your, yours, you, us, they, them, her, him, it, theirs, his, hers, this, these, those, and so forth.

A scripture study technique that has helped me immensely is that when I come to a pronoun I mentally or verbally replace it with the noun. Using this one technique will open many doors of scripture understanding.

In order to substitute a noun for a pronoun, it is helpful to follow an instruction often given to missionaries when they introduce a verse or verses to their investigators. Simply answer three questions—who is speaking, to whom, and about what? Knowing the answers to these three questions will help you to substitute nouns for pronouns automatically when you come to them. For example, in the verses cited above in Doctrine and Covenants 25, helpfully introduced, the teacher might say, "The Lord is speaking *to* Emma Smith *about* being an elect lady."

One of the great chapters on leadership in all scripture comes from the Old Testament (see 1 Samuel 10). In verse 1 the writer is speaking to us about the anointing of Saul as the first king of united Israel, and in it we can apply the technique of substitution. "Then Samuel took a vial of oil, and poured it upon his head, and kissed him, and said, Is it not because the Lord hath anointed thee to be captain over his inheritance?" (1 Samuel 10:1). In order of their appearance, note the pronouns it, his, him, it, thee, his. As we apply the technique of substitution, the verse may read now as follows: "Then Samuel took a vial of oil, and poured [the oil] upon [Saul's] head, and kissed [Saul] and said, Is it [the word *it* is a neuter pronoun, here used as the object of an impersonal verb, hence there is no antecedent] not because the Lord hath anointed [Saul] to be captain over [the Lord's] inheritance?" (1 Samuel 10:1).

This verse blossomed with greater meaning to me by my substituting nouns for pronouns, and from this substituting I likened it to me. Although we do not use oil today in the ordaining and setting apart of leaders, the truths in verse 1 still apply. It is the Lord who calls or anoints through His prophets and other priesthood leaders (see D&C 36:2 and the comments about it earlier in this chapter). It is He who gives His Spirit as we accept an inheritance or a call to serve.

Consider one more example from this great chapter on leadership. In verse 6 Samuel the prophet is speaking and is giving Saul three promises as the leader in Israel, which all leaders can qualify to receive today. There are only three pronouns here—thee, thou, and them. Substituting each for its respective antecedent and creating a list of three promises, we make the verse read as follows (the technique of looking for lists in scriptures is discussed in chapter 6):

1. And the Spirit of the Lord will come upon [Saul],
2. And [Saul] shalt prophesy with [the company of prophets],
3. And [Saul] shalt be turned into another man (1 Samuel 10:6).

By reading the previous verses, you will usually find the noun for which a pronoun stands. In this case the pronoun *them* in the second promise is replaced by the words "a company of prophets," which are found in verse 5. As with verse 1, when I substituted nouns for the pronouns and then inserted my name, I found it easier to liken the verse to me. By doing this I discovered the great truth that every leader—man or woman—in this Church can be the beneficiary of these three great promises.

Following Nephi's example to liken the scriptures to us, I have included two illustrations of 1 Samuel 10:6. Many are the times that these three promises have been and will be fulfilled. For example, as a branch president at the Provo Missionary Training Center I witnessed these promises in every missionary who humbly turned his or her life over to the Lord. One in particular stands out.

When this elder sat in front of me in our first interview, he declared that except for his missionary farewell talk he had never spoken in church. Giving talks terrified him. Also, he had never read the Book of Mormon from cover to cover. He said he did want to serve a mission and was willing to try. Every day of his eight-week stay he worked hard, prayed much, and studied diligently. Many and long were our interviews as he struggled with disappointment and frustration. Several priesthood blessings were given to strengthen him in his resolve and faith. He left the Missionary Training Center after the eight weeks of training. In his farewell talk and testimony to our little branch, I witnessed the power of these three promises. The Spirit of the Lord did come upon him; he prophesied, which according to Revelation 19:10 is to testify of Christ; and he truly was turned into another man.

The above was easy to see and believe as I worked with missionaries, but what about those who live in the wards and stakes of Zion, particularly those who have wandered, those whom we call less active? What evidences are there for the fulfillment of the three promises from Samuel?

While I was serving as bishop, several of our sons and I were reassigned to be home teachers to a less-active couple, wonderful people and long-time neighbors. I say reassigned because years earlier we were called to be their home teachers and then were later transferred to other families. During the first time we worked with them there was never any sign of spiritual awakenings. They were happy to have us come, but "preachy" lessons were more tolerated than welcomed.

The husband was an elder in the Melchizedek Priesthood, but he and his wife had never received the temple ordinances.

For our sons and me, the reassignment was welcomed. We really did love them, and we were genuinely concerned for them.

They were such a good couple that to consider they would not be together forever simply was unthinkable to us. We prayed for them and sought ways to be instruments in the Lord's hands to bless them with the gospel.

Our prayers were answered through their youngest son, a prospective elder in his early twenties who rarely attended church or participated in any of its activities. His contact with the Church through his teen years was through sports and through a few LDS friends.

He met and fell in love with a young lady, a bishop's daughter, who had recently been divorced. When they discussed marriage she told him that she would marry him, but only in the temple. Because I was his bishop, he came to me to learn what he had to do to qualify to go to the temple. We read a few scriptures together and outlined what he must accomplish, and, as his home teachers, my sons and I committed ourselves to help him.

The thought came into my mind, "But what about his parents?" I asked him if he had thought about inviting his parents to go to the temple with them. What a great motivation this might be to help them put their lives in order! He had not done so but liked the idea. I asked him if he wanted to talk to them or should I, hoping of course that he would. He said he would but also asked me to support him and follow up by discussing it with them, knowing that they too would have to make some significant changes in their lives. I shall never forget the sweet experiences that followed.

As the bishop to this couple and to their son, a day or two after my visit with him I visited them in their home and confirmed that he had indeed talked to them on the matter. I rejoiced with their response. They had agreed. They loved their son and saw his desire to change and improve his life. They knew enough about the Church and temples to exercise their faith and find out for themselves if all that the Church stands for is right.

We set up a program over the coming months to prepare them all for the blessings and ordinances of the holy temple. It would require a minimum of two visits a month on our part to review and discuss the basic doctrines of the kingdom. We outlined what the Lord expects of us in terms of personal righteousness—daily prayer and scripture study, Word of Wisdom observance, payment of tithes and offerings, and public righteousness such as attendance at meetings and helping and serving others. They agreed to begin immediately to repent and change.

They worked diligently and kept every commitment. A few months later I witnessed one of the sweetest experiences afforded us in mortality. In the Manti temple, by the authority of the Holy Melchizedek Priesthood, the temple sealer first sealed the son and his beautiful bride, followed by the sealing of his parents. Then he sealed the son to his parents. To cap it off, he then sealed the father to his parents.

The father accepted a calling to be the advisor to the priests quorum. He and I alternated giving lessons. Week after week I witnessed in the life of this fine man the fulfillment of these three great promises from 1 Samuel:

1. And the Spirit of the Lord will come upon [him],
2. And [he] shalt prophesy with [the priests quorum],
3. And shalt be turned into another man (1 Samuel 10:6).

In some references with many pronouns, finding the antecedents requires more effort, as illustrated in the example below. In these verses the Lord is speaking to Nephi and his brothers concerning the great Book of Mormon theme of obedience leading to prosperity. To illustrate this scripture technique, I have written the noun or antecedent following each pronoun.

> And inasmuch as ye [Nephi] shall keep my [the Lord's] commandments, ye [Nephi] shall prosper, and shall be led to a land of promise; yea, even a land which I [the Lord] have prepared for you [Nephi]; yea, a land which is choice above all other lands.
>
> And inasmuch as thy [Nephi's] brethren shall rebel against thee [Nephi], they [Nephi's brothers] shall be cut off from the presence of the Lord.
>
> And inasmuch as thou [Nephi] shalt keep my [the Lord's] commandments, thou [Nephi] shalt be made a ruler and a teacher over thy [Nephi's] brethren.
>
> For behold, in that day that they [Nephi's brothers] shall rebel

against me [the Lord], I [the Lord] will curse them [the brothers] even with a sore curse, and they [the brothers] shall have no power over thy [Nephi's] seed except they [Nephi's seed] shall rebel against me [the Lord] also.

And if it so be that they [Nephi's seed] rebel against me [the Lord], they [the brothers] shall be a scourge unto thy [Nephi's] seed, to stir them [Nephi's seed] up in the ways of remembrance. (1 Nephi 2:20–24.)

Without working carefully through these verses looking for pronouns, as illustrated in these passages from Nephi, it is no wonder that our daughter expressed her frustrations with "I don't know who is speaking, to whom, and about what." This simple exercise of substituting nouns for pronouns made all the difference for her and our other children. This technique is so much a part of me that as I study and search I automatically replace pronouns with their antecedent.

One of the most difficult challenges in applying this technique is that the antecedent is not always clear. An illustration of unclear antecedents is in the following example dealing with the priesthood and the ordinances (see D&C 84:19–22). My search began one day with the word *this* from verse 22: "For without *this* no man can see the face of God, even the Father, and live" (emphasis added). I said to myself, "But what is the antecedent for *this*? I want to see the face of the Father and I want to live eternally with Him and with my family." For my own benefit and eventual exaltation, I wanted to know what *this* refers to. Note also that the pronoun is singular, not the plural word *these*.

The closest antecedent is the phrase "the power of godliness" in verse 21. As I studied further, I was not certain that this phrase was the answer. In verses 20 and 21 it is clear that in the ordinances—baptism, confirmation, sacrament, priesthood

20 "Therefore, in the ordinances thereof, the power of godliness is manifest.

ordinations, endowment, and sealing—the power of godliness is manifest, and without the ordinances and the authority of the priest-hood, the power of godliness is not manifest. Without *this* no man can see the face of God, the Father, and live. Furthermore, Moses taught *this* to the children of Israel (see verse 23). To capture these principles, my scriptures are marked as shown.

21 "And without the (1) ordinances thereof, and (2) the authority of the priesthood, (3) the power of godliness is not manifest unto men in the flesh;

22 "For without <u>this</u> no man can see the face of God, even the Father, and live."

What is the antecedent for *this*? A possible answer is the complete idea that ordinances are done in the authority of the priesthood, which can result in the power of godliness—and without all of *this*, no man can see the face of God.

The Book of Mormon is the word of God. It truly is a translation. It was translated by the gift and power of God. One evidence that it is a translation is supported by trying to connect pronouns with their antecedents. Making such connections is not always clear or easy. The Prophet Joseph Smith did not stop to ensure that these connections were clear. He simply translated text as it appeared. Once translated, he did not make edits to ensure that pronouns and antecedents were always clear.

An example of this fact is found in the first eleven verses of 3 Nephi 21. A major doctrinal message in the first part of this chapter is that the Book of Mormon is the instrument for the gathering of Israel, and it will be given to Israel from the Gentiles. These truths became much more clear to me through a careful review of pronouns and their antecedents in 3 Nephi 21.

The words *these things* appear frequently throughout the Book of Mormon. One of the antecedents for these two words is the Book of Mormon or what is in it (see 1 Nephi 13:35; 1 Nephi 19:12, 18, 19, 22; Alma 37:8, 9, 14–18; Mormon 5:12; 8:25; Moroni 10:3–4). In 3 Nephi 21 the phrase "these things" appears in verses 1, 2, 3, 4, and 7. It has two different uses: one is a general use as in verses 1 and 7, and the other use is specific, referring to the Book of Mormon (see verses 2, 3, 4, and 7). Because I desire to emphasize a technique in the verses below, each pronoun is followed by its antecedent.

v. 1   When these things [what is taught in chapter 20] shall be about to take place.

v. 2   When these things which I [the Lord] shall declare unto you [my people, Israel], and which I shall declare unto you hereafter, i.e., the teachings of the Savior in the Book of Mormon.

v. 3   When these things [the Book of Mormon] shall be made known unto them [the Gentiles] of the Father, and shall come forth of the Father from them [the Gentiles] unto you [my people, the remnant of the house of Israel].

v. 4   For it is wisdom in the Father that they [the Gentiles] should be established in this land, and be set up as a free people by the power of the Father, that these things [the Book of Mormon] might come forth from them [the Gentiles] unto a remnant of your seed [remnant of Israel], that the covenant of the Father may be fulfilled which he hath covenanted with his people, O house of Israel.

v. 7   And when these things [the truths taught in verses 1–6] come to pass that thy seed [remnant of Israel] shall begin to know these things [the Book of Mormon]—it [the coming forth of these things, the Book of Mormon] shall be a sign unto them [remnant of Israel], that they [remnant of Israel] may know that the work of the Father hath already commenced unto the fulfilling of the covenant which he [the Father] hath made unto the people who are of the house of Israel.

v. 10   But behold, the life of my [the Lord's] servant [probably Joseph Smith] shall be in my hand; therefore they [the Gentiles] shall not hurt him [my servant], although he [my servant] shall be marred because of them [the Gentiles]. Yet I [the Lord] will heal him [my servant], for I [the Lord] will show unto them [the Gentiles] that my [the Lord's] wisdom is greater than the cunning of the devil.

v. 11   Therefore it shall come to pass that whosoever will not believe in my [the Lord's] words, who am Jesus Christ, which the Father shall cause him [my servant] to bring forth unto the Gentiles, and shall give unto him [my servant] power that he [my servant] shall bring them [these things—the Book of Mormon] forth unto the Gentiles, (it shall be done even as Moses said) they [the Gentiles] shall be cut off from among my [the Lord's] people who are of the covenant.

As I get into the flow of a verse and it is abundantly clear who is speaking to whom, I do not verbally or silently include each one.

This technique is not an end but rather a means to an end. As I read and study the scriptures, the technique has become so much a part of me that, either silently or aloud, automatically I make nouns replace pronouns. Where appropriate I insert my name in a verse. Principles of substitution help me to discover hidden treasures in the scriptures.

Over the years I have kept a list of scripture references where the antecedent is not always clear, and I share it with you should you like to practice this scripture study technique on your own, looking at some examples where more effort is required to find the antecedent.

1 Corinthians 15:24	3 Nephi 19:28
1 Nephi 22:6	Ether 8:10
2 Nephi 5:25	Moroni 6:2
Words of Mormon 1:17–18	D&C 42:80–93
Alma 11:20	D&C 45:36
Helaman 9:18–19	D&C 109:46
3 Nephi 15:16–24	Moses 5:30

But the technique of substituting is only the first of several techniques, the next one being lists.

6

Lists

In our day lists are a part of our lives; for example, Christmas shopping lists that never seem to end, and market lists. Items purchased at the market end up in the kitchen, where they are often subjected to a list outlined in a recipe.

Another example is planners. Into planners go lists of goals—short-range, intermediate, and long-range. Furthermore, for each day of the week there are "to do" lists, tasks that are prioritized and placed in sequences. And so it goes. Our lives really are impacted by lists.

My study of the scriptures has taught me that lists abound in the scriptures, some by careful design and others because the messages simply fall into an orderly sequence.

To me the benefits of lists are as follows:

1. Identifying them causes me to stop reading the scriptures and start studying and searching them.
2. Many truths are arranged in logical order, which facilitates reasoning. The Lord said he would "reason with you that you may understand" (D&C 50:12; see also 2 Nephi 31:3).
3. A list helps me to retain and recall.
4. Application is enhanced because I can act on or do each item listed.
5. A list provides me with an outline for talks and lessons.

While all five benefits are important, the first four contribute to and lay the foundation for number five. This last benefit—talks and lessons—is perhaps my most-used purpose for scripture lists and therefore the most important to me. Many of the lists marked in my scriptures are instant talks and lesson outlines. For example, in the previous chapter on substitution, the three promises that Samuel gave to Saul have served as the basis for talks and lessons. With an illustration for each of the three promises, I have an instant talk or lesson.

How to Identify a List

Many lists have their own enumeration already, such as many verses in Proverbs or the fourth article of faith. Closely related to cardinal numbers (one, two, three, four, and so forth) are categories or groups of items or elements such as those listed in Articles of Faith 1:6, 7, 12, 13. Very often these are placed in a verse in a series and are separated by commas or the conjunctions *and* or *or.*

As will be seen throughout this chapter, some lists are conceptually centered and others are word driven. An example of a conceptual list would be the Ten Commandments or the Beatitudes. A word list is simply words in a series separated by commas, such as "faith, hope, charity and love, with an eye single to the glory of God" (D&C 4:5) or by the repetition of a word. Some lists may be a combination of the two, such as the Beatitudes, where each one begins with the same words "blessed are" followed by different doctrinal concepts.

Well-known Lists

Perhaps the most well-known list in scripture is the Ten Commandments. Some scholars like to break this list into two smaller lists, the first four dealing with our relationship with God and the last six with our relations as mortals.

Continuing with another example from the Old Testament is this list from Proverbs. Also, note how I have marked	"These six things doth the LORD hate: yea, seven [are] an abomination unto him: (1) A proud look, (2) a

this reference. Instead of shading the verses, I simply wrote
the number by each item.

lying tongue, and (3) hands
that shed innocent blood,
    (4) An heart that deviseth
wicked imaginations, (5) feet
that be swift in running to
mischief,
    (6) A false witness that
speaketh lies, and (7) he that
soweth discord among
brethren" (Proverbs 6:16–19).

In latter-day scriptures one of the most well-known lists is the thirteen articles of faith. Several of the articles of faith are also written in the form of a list, such as number four: "We believe that the first principles and ordinances of the Gospel are: first . . . ," followed by the four great truths of faith in Jesus Christ, repentance, baptism, and the gift of the Holy Ghost. Articles six and seven also contain a list. The sixth includes five Church officers, and in the seventh six spiritual gifts are identified. See also articles 12 and 13 for other examples of lists.

In the previous chapter,
on substituting, I identified a
simple list of three promises
to all who have a calling to
serve. In my scriptures that
verse is marked as shown at
the right.

"And (1) the Spirit of the
Lord will come upon thee,
and (2) thou shalt prophesy
with them, and (3) shalt be
turned into another man" (1
Samuel 10:6).

Lists of items separated by the word and *or a comma.* Many lists are categories of items separated by the conjunction *and* or a comma. An illustration of this kind of list, and one of my favorites, is in Doctrine and Covenants section 4.

The introduction to the section alerts you to a possible list with "Godly attributes [that] qualify them [the Lord's ministers] for the ministry" (see D&C 4, synopsis). The attributes in question are in verses 5 and 6 as follows:

Verse 5
1. Faith
2. Hope
3. Charity
4. Love

Verse 6
5. Faith
6. Virtue
7. Knowledge
8. Temperance
9. Patience
10. Brotherly kindness
11. Godliness
12. Charity
13. Humility
14. Diligence

The Book of Mormon is the key to understanding the Atonement, which cannot be taught without including these three great truths—merits, mercy, grace. Each of the three is separated from the others by a comma and by the word *and* in the verse shown to the right.

"Wherefore, how great the importance to make these things known unto the inhabitants of the earth, that they may know that there is no flesh that can dwell in the presence of God, save it be through (1) the merits, and (2) mercy, and (3) grace of the Holy Messiah . . . " (2 Nephi 2:8).

Another aspect of the Atonement is what the Savior experienced in the Garden of Gethsemane and on the cross, which led the angel to tell King Benjamin that it caused Jesus to bleed from every pore. In this list of five truths, note the use of the comma as well as the conjunction <u>and</u>.

"And lo, he shall suffer (1) temptations, and (2) pain of body, (3) hunger, (4) thirst, and (5) fatigue" (Mosiah 3:7).

To receive the benefits of the Atonement we must do our part. Note the strength of these four words (verbs)—*repent, forsake, humble,* and *ask.*

"And again, believe that ye must (1) repent of your sins and (2) forsake them, and (3) humble yourselves before God; and (4) ask in sincerity of heart that he would forgive you" (Mosiah 4:10).

More information is given that tells us what we must do to be forgiven. The repetition of the word *their* with the first and the third truth, as well as the word *and* and commas, helped me to identify this list.

"And no unclean thing can enter into his kingdom; therefore nothing entereth into his rest save it be those who have washed their garments in my blood, because of (1) their faith, and (2) the repentance of all their sins, and (3) their faithfulness unto the end" (3 Nephi 27:19).

Note in this reference that under the third truth there is a sublist of an "a" and a "b." In some references you will find sublists. Did you notice that each truth in the list begins with the same word—*to: to* tremble, *to* bleed, and *to* suffer? Each truth is also separated by the word *and* and a comma.

"Which suffering caused myself, even God, the greatest of all, (1) to tremble because of pain, and (2) to bleed at every pore, and (3) to suffer both (a) body and (b) spirit . . . " (D&C 19:18).

Although not used as often in the scriptures, the word *or* can also help you to identify a list. It can be as simple as two truths or more, as seen in the following two examples.

Although this is a short list, each word is eternally significant.

"Think not that I am come to destroy (1) the law or (2) the prophets" (3 Nephi 12:17).

This beautiful list in 3 Nephi 17:7 illustrates the compassion and mercy of the Savior. Note that two verses later there is a list of six groups of people that Jesus healed (see 3 Nephi 17:9).

"Have ye any that are sick among you? Bring them hither. Have ye any that are (1) lame, or (2) blind, or (3) halt, or (4) maimed, or (5) leprous, or (6) that are withered, or (7) that are deaf, or (8) that are afflicted in any manner? Bring them hither and I will heal them, for I have compassion upon you; my bowels are filled with mercy." (3 Nephi 17:7.)

One more verse illustrates the use of the word *or*. Note, however, that in this one each item in the list is more than a single word and that each item in the list begins with the same word *by*.

"Yea, wo unto him that shall deny the revelations of the Lord, and that shall say the Lord no longer worketh (1) by revelation, or (2) by prophecy, or (3) by gifts, or (4) by tongues, or (5) by healings, or (6) by the power of the Holy Ghost!" (3 Nephi 29:6.)

Remember that lists are not an end but rather a means to an end. These lists help you to study and search instead of only read the scriptures. They are to help you seek the deeper and more complete meaning in the scriptures. By doing so you will come to know the Father and the Son and draw closer to them. You will make the scriptures more fully a part of your life. By so doing you will place yourself on that path that leads to life eternal, the greatest gift of God.

Lists of items that begin with the same word or word groups. Many lists are readily found because of the repetition of the same word. Few chapters in the Book of Mormon better illustrate the power of the word than Alma 32. In this chapter Alma invited his hearers, and us today, to "experiment upon [the word]" (Alma

32:27). In the next verse he compared the word to a seed. If it is a good seed or a true seed, three results will follow, each one standing out because of the words "it beginneth to." "(1) It beginneth to enlarge my soul; (2) yea, it beginneth to enlighten my understanding, (3) yea, it beginneth to be delicious to me" (Alma 32:28).

Few scripture references contain three more important truths about the ways in which we can know the truth of the word. Enlarging generally involves feelings such as joy, happiness, peace, and love. Something wonderful is happening inside you that is seeking release or expression. Enlightening has to do with the "lights turning on" spiritually and intellectually. The word is light, and light is truth, and truth is Spirit (see D&C 84:45). You may have silently or verbally said something like "oh" or "ah hah." When this enlightening occurs, you may see something in the verses that makes sense, sounds true, and is completely reasonable. Finally, words that enlarge and that enlighten are also delicious. Something that is delicious is sought for again and again. You hunger and thirst for it. The Prophet Joseph Smith said:

> This is good doctrine. It tastes good. I can taste the principles of eternal life, and so can you. They are given to me by the revelations of Jesus Christ; and I know that when I tell you these words of eternal life as they are given to me, you taste them, and I know that you believe them. You say honey is sweet, and so do I. I can also taste the spirit of eternal life. I know it is good; and when I tell you of these things which were given me by inspiration of the Holy Spirit, you are bound to receive them as sweet, and rejoice more and more. (*Teachings of the Prophet Joseph Smith,* p. 355.)

A short two-item list to support the imperative need to preach the word is in Alma 42:31. Note that each of the two truths begins with the word *that.* The worth of souls is great (see D&C 18:10–16), and because they are of such great worth we declare words

"And now, O my son, ye are called of God to preach the word unto this people. And now, my son, go thy way, declare the word with truth and soberness, (1) that thou mayest bring souls unto repentance, (2) that the great plan of mercy may have claim upon

to them and thus see the fulfillment of these two purposes.

The repetition of the pronoun *it* in 2 Nephi 33:4–5 opened my eyes and heart to Nephi's explanation of four purposes for preserving the records. Here is an opportunity to review and apply the technique of substitution. The pronoun *it* is used four times—*it* persuadeth, *it* maketh known, *it* speaketh and persuadeth, and *it* speaketh. But what is the antecedent for *it*? The answer is "the words which I have written in weakness." Note also that there are two subpoints under the third *it,* and two of the four are the same as two of the three declared purposes of the Book of Mormon: (1) "what great things the Lord hath done for their fathers;" and (2) "to the convincing of the Jew and Gentile that Jesus is the Christ" (see Book of Mormon title page, paragraph 2).

Several lists are found in Mosiah 4. One of them I discovered because of the repetition of the words *ye shall* and *ye will.* Another major discovery was that these eighteen

them." (Alma 42:31.)

"And the words which I have written in weakness will be made strong unto them; for (1) it persuadeth them to do good; (2) it maketh known unto them of their fathers; and (3) it speaketh of Jesus, and persuadeth them (a) to believe in him, and (b) to endure to the end, which is life eternal.

"And (4) it speaketh harshly against sin . . . " (2 Nephi 33:4–5.)

"I would that ye should remember and always (1) retain in remembrance, (a) the greatness of God, and (b) your own nothingness, and (c) his goodness and long-suffering

items are results, not commands. Although they can be and often are quoted by teachers and speakers as commands or what we ought to do, especially as parents in teaching and rearing children, the precise use of each item is a result or consequence. The key to this insight came because of my looking for the antecedent of the pronoun *this* in verse 12—"if ye do this."

towards you, unworthy creatures, and (2) humble yourselves even in the depths of humility, (3) calling on the name of the Lord daily, and (4) standing steadfastly in the faith of that which is to come, which was spoken by the mouth of the angel" (Mosiah 4:11).

The word *this* refers to a list of truths we are to follow. At the end of verse 11 is the reminder to stand fast in "the faith of that which is to come, which was spoken by the mouth of the angel." What was spoken by the mouth of the angel? All of Mosiah chapter 3 is a glorious and wondrous doctrinal explanation of Jesus Christ and His atonement, including the marvelous and oft-quoted verse 19 about the natural man becoming a Saint through the atonement of Jesus Christ. If we do *this*, there are 18 promises or results, if you include the subpoints. (The introductory line of each subpoint is not counted as a separate item.) I have grouped them according to verse and "ye shall" and "ye will":

Verse 12

1. Ye shall always rejoice.
2. [Ye shall] be filled with the love of God.
3. [Ye shall] always retain a remission of your sins.
4. Ye shall grow in the knowledge of the glory of him that created you, or in the knowledge of that which is just and true.

Verse 13

5. Ye will not have a mind
   a. To injure one another, but
   b. To live peaceably, and

c. To render to every man according to that which is his due.

Verse 14

6. Ye will not suffer your children that they
   a. Go hungry, or
   b. Naked.
7. Neither will ye suffer that they
   a. Transgress the laws of God, and
   b. Fight and quarrel[1] one with another, and
   c. Serve the devil.

Verse 15

8. Ye will teach them to walk in the ways of truth and soberness;
9. Ye will teach them to love one another and
10. [Ye will teach them] to serve[2] one another.

Verse 16

11. Ye yourselves will succor those that stand in need of succor;
12. Ye will administer of your substance unto him that standeth in need; and
13. Ye will not suffer that the beggar putteth up his petition to you in vain, and turn him out to perish.

Should you want to have more experience with this scripture study technique, the following references include words that are repeated, resulting in a list. Obviously, it is not a comprehensive list and it comes only from the Book of Mormon. To help focus your attention on the key word that is repeated, it follows each reference along with the number of items I have identified.

---

1. To me, *fight* and *quarrel* are synonyms. Each could be a separate item in the list, but because they are synonymous I choose to keep them as one item.
2. Love and serve are closely related but doctrinally are two separate truths; therefore I choose to number each one as a separate item on my list of "ye wills" and "ye shalls."

2 Nephi 3:12	Confounding and other gerunds ("ing" words)—4.
2 Nephi 4:20–23	Hath—7
2 Nephi 11:2, 4–6	Delighteth—5
Mosiah 15:8–9	Having, giving, being, standing—8
Alma 9:19–22	Having—14
Alma 13:28–29	Becoming and having—4
Alma 17:2–3	They—8
Alma 26:22	"eth" words—repenteth, exerciseth, bringeth, and prayeth—4
Alma 26:22	It—3
Alma 32:42	Your—3 (see similar lists in vv. 41 and 43)
Alma 34:37–41	That—14
Alma 38:3	Thy—4
Helaman 12:1–3	We can, may, see—4
3 Nephi 11:15	Did—4 (This list begins following the phrase "one by one.")
3 Nephi 20:25	Ye are—3
3 Nephi 29:2–4, 8, 9	Ye need not—5
Mormon 7:2–5	Know ye—4
Ether 8:26	That—4
Moroni 10:3, 4, 7, 8, 18, 19, 27, 30	I would exhort—8 (Note that vv. 8 and 27 do not include the word *would* but nonetheless convey the same emphasis and should be included in the list.)

Conceptual Lists

Each writer of the Book of Mormon was faithful to the threefold purpose as declared in the second paragraph of the title page, especially to the convincing of Jews and Gentiles that Jesus Christ is the

"And at that day shall the remnant of our seed know (1) that they are of the house of Israel, and (2) that they are the covenant people of the Lord; and then shall they (3) know and come to the knowl-

Son of God the Father. Nephi, the first writer of the Book of Mormon, elaborated on those three purposes when he taught his brothers about the scattering and the gathering.

edge of their forefathers, and (4) also to the knowledge of the gospel of their Redeemer, which was ministered unto their fathers by him; wherefore, (5) they shall come to the knowledge of their Redeemer and the very points of his doctrine, that (6) they may know how to come unto him and be saved" (1 Nephi 15:14).

Although this list of six truths has some repetition of a word such as *know* and *that,* the entire list is found only through careful study and examination, resulting in a wonderful doctrinal, conceptual list.

As members of The Church of Jesus Christ of Latter-day Saints we seek revelation. We want light and truth. Nephi did also. He received a marvelous vision, similar to that of John the Revelator (see 1 Nephi 14:25–26), that is contained in 1 Nephi 11–14. He taught us four truths that are prerequisites to obtaining such light and truth, which was to see the things that his father had seen:

1. After I had *desired to know* the things that my father had seen,
2. And *believing that the Lord was able to make them known* unto me,
3. As I *sat pondering* in mine heart . . .
4. . . . I *believe all the words* of my father (1 Nephi 11:1, 5).

This divine process was followed by the Prophet Joseph Smith. He desired to know things (which Church was true—JS-H 1:10), he believed the Lord was able to make them known to him (JS-H 1:13), he reflected again and again on James 1:5 (JS-H 1:12), and he believed the words of God the Father (JS-H 1:12–13).

In the next example, a formula of three truths can contribute to our spiritual growth and self-esteem. "Seeing that our merciful God has given us so great knowledge concerning these things, (1) let us remember him [our merciful God], and (2) [let us] lay aside our sins, and (3) [let us] not hang down our heads" (2 Nephi 10:20).

Although the words *let us* are not repeated with the second and third item, they help me to clearly see the three truths if I repeat them. These three truths really do work. They are very doable. The first one—to remember Him—is part of the baptismal covenant and is renewed each week when we partake of the sacrament. Sins can be set aside. Finally, the simple practice of holding our heads up has great power and strength.

These three truths are indeed solutions to self-esteem and spiritual growth. As a student at Brigham Young University, occasionally I would sit on a bench and watch people walk by. Of special interest to me was to observe those whose chins were on their chest, so to speak. Their heads hung down, symbolic of a possible burden on their shoulders. I saw similar heads when presiding over a mission. The missionaries who were carrying burdens were often easy to detect by the way they carried their heads. To them and to me today I want to shout the words of Jacob: let us remember Him, let us lay aside our sins, and let us not hang down our heads!

These beautiful truths from Jacob lead to a related list in the book of Alma. This list is "triggered" by the words "the Lord did visit us with assurances that he would deliver us" (Alma 58:11). How did they know of these assurances? There are three of them. Also, each one is introduced with the word *did*. Having such assurances helps us keep our chins off our

"Yea, and it came to pass that the Lord our God did visit us with assurances that he would deliver us; yea, insomuch that (1) he did speak peace to our souls, and (2) did grant unto us great faith, and (3) did cause us that we should hope for our deliverance in him" (Alma 58:11).

chests and hold our heads up
because of our faith in God.

Lists of Truths in a Sequence that Illustrate Processes

Truths are often placed in a list, beginning with the very first verse of the Book of Mormon. Nephi gave us an excellent outline or list of what to include in a journal.

1. "I, Nephi"

   Start with your name.

2. "Having been born of goodly parents"

   Write about your parents and why they are and were "goodly." It is hard to talk about parents without also talking about other family members.

3. "I was taught somewhat in all the learning of my father"

   What have your father and mother taught you? Is it recorded in your journal? Notice the wisdom in the phrase "taught somewhat in all the learning." Parents wisely teach you *somewhat in all* they know; however, valuable lessons come through your own experiences and from others.

4. "Having seen many ᵉafflictions in the course of my days"

   All journals should include afflictions through which the writer passes. Nephi was faithful in including many of his afflictions, as were many of the prophets. We learn from them the valuable lessons of life. The superscript "e" preceding the word *afflictions* leads you to the footnote "TG Affliction; Blessing; God, Gifts of."

5. "Having been highly favored of the Lord"

Note the word *nevertheless* that connects afflictions with being highly favored in all my days. The Lord is mindful of us. Elder Boyd K. Packer has reminded us that "disappointment, sorrow, and pain are all flames for the refiner's fire, but they are to temper us only and not to consume us."

6. "Having had a great knowledge of the goodness . . . of God"

Note that Nephi said he had a *great* knowledge, not an ordinary but a *great* knowledge of God's goodness. After having read 1 Nephi and 2 Nephi, we know what he meant. Your journal should also include your great knowledge of the goodness of God. It is probably in the atonement of Jesus Christ that we best see the goodness of God (see 2 Nephi 9:10; 2 Nephi 26:27–28, 33; Jacob 1:7; Mosiah 4:5–6, 11; Alma 12:32; Moroni 8:3). All journals should have regular entries of one's feelings towards the Father and the Son and the infinite and eternal atonement as it impacts one's life.

7. "Having . . . a great knowledge of . . . the mysteries of God"

A good synonym for the word *mysteries* is revelations. All receive revelations. Of course we do not ask that they be published or included in the Doctrine and Covenants. Revelations, impressions, and spiritual thoughts are an important part of journals. There may be some, however, that are so personal and sacred that, if you record them, they must be safeguarded where only you can review them.

"Therefore I make a record of my proceedings in my days." Following Nephi's example, we make a record of our proceedings in our days and include in our record some if not all the things such as Nephi included in his. These seven suggestions for a journal illustrate the value of lists in scripture. Such lists are found through studying, pondering, and praying to be taught. The word *therefore* near the end of the verse helped me study it more carefully because this word is often used to set up a cause and effect relationship. I asked myself the question, "What ideas preceded the word *therefore* that caused Nephi to say it?"

How do I find these other kinds of lists? First and foremost, I strive to prayerfully study and ponder the scriptures. This causes me to examine words, sentences, verses, and entire chapters. Many of these other lists are found through a micro-view and a macro-view. The micro-view is compared to taking a magnifying glass and carefully studying each word, sentence, and verse. This micro-view approach is illustrated in the previous chapter and in the illustrations thus far in this chapter.

The macro-view requires that you step back and look at the events and truths from a distance. Most chapter synopses in our scriptures are in fact macro-views.

For an example of a micro-view, continue on with the first chapter of 1 Nephi, and notice a less obvious list in the final two verses. What led me to identify this list of three truths? I found in verse 20 the statement "they also sought [to take] his life." Notice the word *also*. What did that refer to? It implied at least one other item in a series. I studied backwards in the same verse and in the preceding verse and found that the Jews at first mocked Lehi. When mocking produced no results they became angry, and they followed this by seeking to take his life, as had been done with other prophets before him.

Now look at 1 Nephi 1 and the first few verses from chapter 2[3] from a distance, looking for major events such as these four: (1) Lehi prayed; (2) he received a vision or an answer to his prayer; (3) he was challenged; and (4) following the challenges,

---

3. Note that while verses and chapters are very helpful tools, they can limit us in our search for truths if we abruptly end an idea at the end of one chapter, assuming that it is complete, when in fact the ideas continue into the next chapter.

additional light and truth came. These four profound truths are
found in the lives of most prophets and great Saints. Furthermore,
they are illustrated in the life and mission of Jesus Christ. These
four are a true pattern for spiritual growth.

A True Pattern for Spiritual Growth

Situation	Jesus Christ	Joseph Smith	Moses	Lehi
Sensed sacred responsibility and sought help, communion with God	Went into wilderness to be with God (JS-M 4:1)	Which church is true? (JS-H 1:8–10)	Caught up into a mountain to be with God (Moses 1:1)	Prayed for his people (1 Nephi 1:5)
Enlightened—revelation and instruction given	Communed with God (JS-M 4:2)	Answer came that if you lack wisdom ask God (JS-H 1:11–12)	Saw world, ends of it, and people on it (Moses 1:8)	Saw and heard much (1 Nephi 1:6)
Challenged and tried—intense opposition	Satan tempted Him (Matt. 4:3–10)	Seized upon by unseen power (JS-H 1:15)	Satan confronted him (Moses 1:12–22)	Jews mocked, and sought his life (1 Nephi 1:19–20)
Strengthened—victory entitles you to proceed with increased light and truth	Angels came and ministered (Matt. 4:11)	Father and Son appeared to him (JS-H 1:17–19)	Filled with Holy Ghost and saw much (Moses 1:24–42)	Had a dream and was comforted (1 Nephi 2:1)

Another illustration of this macro-view that includes a list is
found in Doctrine and Covenants 138:1–6, 11, 25, 28–29. This
list is seen by carefully studying how President Joseph F. Smith
studied and *pondered* scriptures.

v. 1	He sat in his room. Sit still with your body functions at rest. Eliminate distractions and sit erect. (I learned as a missionary and as a mission president that missionaries who, after getting up and praying and perhaps even dressing, lie on their beds to study are soon asleep.)
vv. 1–4	He pondered and reflected upon the *scriptures* and specific truths in them.
v. 5	Engage the mind. Use all your mental and spiritual powers. Pray vocally and in your heart for light and truth.
v. 6	Open and read, study, and search the scriptures. Have available other written materials, such as talks by latter-day prophets, dictionaries, and other resource material. Do not overlook pen and paper.
v. 6	Leave your heart and mind open so that you might be "greatly impressed."
vv. 25, 28–29	Marvel and wonder. Ask questions like how, why, in what way, how does this relate to . . . , why is this so?

Lists and the divine authenticity of the Book of Mormon. One of the most impressive lists in the Book of Mormon is in Helaman 3:14. In this verse are eighteen *ands*. This verse stands as a witness to the divinity of the Book of Mormon. It came to light through the following account.

Some years ago the First Presidency and Quorum of the Twelve authorized the translation of the Book of Mormon into Arabic. It is important to remember that the Book of Mormon was translated into English from what is called "reformed Egyptian" (see 1 Nephi 1:2; Mormon 9:32). Arabic is spoken in Egypt; consequently, the task of translating the Book of Mormon from English into Arabic consisted of translating it into the language closest to its original, an interesting task.

Those involved in the translation reported that they found unusual sentence constructions that in English sound awkward but are very natural in Arabic. One example was the noun followed by a prepositional phrase, such as *rod of iron* and *plates of brass*. Not once throughout the Book of Mormon do we find the words *iron rod* or *brass plates*.

The phrase *river of water* is another strange concept. Are not all rivers made of water? Not to Semitic people. They are also familiar with rivers of sand. How could Joseph Smith have known that?

Elder Russell M. Nelson has reported the following concerning the translation of the Book of Mormon into Arabic, particularly the translation of Helaman 3:14:

> Sister Nelson and I have a close friend and former neighbor, Sami Hanna, who was born in Egypt. He is a scholar with special expertise in Semitic languages. As a linguistic exercise, he translated the Book of Mormon from English into Arabic. The exercise converted him to the divinity of the Book of Mormon. Among the many linguistic features that convinced him of the book's divinity was this unusual sentence in Helaman, chapter 3, verse 14. This would hardly be an expression of a 24-year-old man from the New York frontier:
>
> "But behold, a hundredth part of the proceedings of this people, yea, the account of the Lamanites and of the Nephites, and their wars, and contentions, and dissensions, and their preaching, and their prophecies, and their shipping and their building of ships, and their building of temples, and of synagogues and their sanctuaries, and their righteousness, and their wickedness, and their murders, and their robbings, and their plundering, and all manner of abominations and whoredoms, cannot be contained in this work" (Helaman 3:14).
>
> That single sentence has eighteen *ands*. Now, if you were a teacher of English you might tend to downgrade the composition of that sentence. Yet my scholarly Egyptian friend said that every one of those *ands* was an important element in the construction of that sentence, allowing his translation to flow smoothly back to a Semitic language. ("A Treasured Testament," *Ensign*, July 1993, p. 63.)

There are other verses in the Book of Mormon where this pattern is seen. In each case a list is preserved (see Enos 1:21; Jarom 1:8; Alma 26:29; 43:17–20; 3 Nephi 30:2). The doctrinal significance of each list of *ands* may not compare in importance to the words following each *and*, but they illustrate the truth that lists abound in the scriptures, and, more important, they bear witness of the divine origin of the Book of Mormon.

Summary

Finding and using lists from the scriptures is not an end, but rather a means to an end. They are simply tools that reflect your intensity of studying, searching, and pondering the scriptures. This scripture study technique will lead you to a height and breadth and depth of truth heretofore unknown to you. It will lead you to increase your faith in and testimony of the Father and the Son and the great plan of happiness. It will lead you on a path of obedience that will enable you to return and live with them in the family unit forever.

7

Definitions

One of the marvelous aspects of the holy scriptures is that they can be enjoyed by all people at all age levels. Little children who are just beginning to talk can feel and know things spiritually as they hear scripture stories or see illustrations of them. When we ask if they understood what they heard, simple statements such as "This teaches us to be good," or "Heavenly Father and Jesus love us," come from their mouths and hearts. They keep doctrine simple and pure. Little ones may not understand many of the "big, long" words, but they know and feel spiritual things. As these little children grow into youth and adulthood, by study they will increase their vocabulary and with it develop a greater and deeper appreciation for the word of the Lord.

When we humbly, prayerfully, and reverently take the holy scriptures into our hands and exercise faith, we can understand these holy words and their meanings. Nephi "was taught somewhat in all the learning of [his] father" (1 Nephi 1:1). "I, Nephi, having heard all the words of my father . . . , was desirous also that I might see, and hear, and know of these things, by the power of the Holy Ghost . . . . For he that diligently seeketh shall find; and the mysteries of God shall be unfolded unto them by the power of the Holy Ghost, as well in these times as in times of old, as well in times of old as in times to come." (1 Nephi 10:17, 19.)

Although some word studies reveal that reading levels for the scriptures vary from as low as a seventh-grade level on up to beginning college levels, truths from scriptures can be learned, loved, and lived by all at all levels. This is brought about through the power of the Spirit, who is our teacher (see 2 Nephi 33:1;

74

D&C 18:34–36; 36:2; 50:14). To learn from the scriptures and the Spirit we must be humble and teachable. We must seek, ask, knock, and search.

While the scriptures can be loved and enjoyed by all, it is important to recognize that for some people, understanding them is not easy. For example, some studies reveal that in some parts of the world illiteracy runs as high as 50 to 75 percent. Functional illiteracy, the inability to read above a fourth-grade level, may be as high as 25 to 30 percent in many states of the United States. However, functional illiteracy is not the only factor; there are other learning or reading disorders.

Because the scriptures are written on a higher reading level than some people's reading ability, these individuals may find the scriptures a great challenge. They may avoid the scriptures. Some may seek and search and pray, but they still experience frustration simply because the words are beyond their comprehension ability. In their hearts, they may say, "I just don't understand," or they may ask, "What does this word mean?"

It certainly was not the intention of the prophets to make the scriptures difficult or beyond the spiritual and intellectual reach of those who want to know and understand them. I recommend, therefore, a scripture study technique that will keep scriptures simple and on a level that will facilitate learning and understanding and will help students love and live the scriptures. This technique is to explain the meaning of words—define them.

Principles and Defining Words

One of the values, if not the main value, of defining words is the learning of principles. A principle is an unchanging truth, an eternal law, a fundamental belief. It is a foundation for other truths. Our conduct grows out of our understanding of correct principles. An oft-quoted statement concerning correct principles is the following:

> What is it that will enable one man to govern his fellows aright? It is just as Joseph Smith said to a certain man who asked him, "How do you govern such a vast people as this?" "Oh," says Joseph,

"it is very easy." "'Why," says the man "but we find it very difficult." "But," said Joseph, "it is very easy, for I teach the people correct principles, and they govern themselves." (John Taylor, *The Gospel Kingdom,* p. 323.)

The Lord commanded, "And again, the elders, priests and teachers of this church shall teach the *principles* of my gospel, which are in the Bible and the Book of Mormon" (D&C 42:12; emphasis added). Principles are found in the scriptures. Our challenge is find them, learn them, love them, and live them.

One of the classic illustrations of this truth is defining the first three key words from Doctrine and Covenants 121:43: "*Reproving betimes* with *sharpness . . . .*" One day while reading this verse, I realized that I did not know the meaning of the word *betimes*. I turned to a dictionary and found that it is an archaic word meaning early, promptly, quickly, before it is too late; to be timely, at the right time; at the right season. Substituting these synonyms for the word *betimes*, I read the line again, "reproving early, promptly, quickly, at the right time, and so forth, and to do it with sharpness." I knew that I had discovered a significant principle. When reproving is needed, it should be done as indicated, lest the act, transgression, or sin become ingrained.

Having come to the realization of this great principle, I asked myself if I knew the meaning of the other two words—*reproving* and *sharpness*. Again I turned to a dictionary, looked up each, and discovered the following:

Reprove — rebuke, reprimand or criticize or blame someone for a fault; it also suggests a kindly intent to correct a fault.
Sharply — curtly, pointedly, severely.

The word *reprove* can connote two extremes—harshness and softness. To see this contrast, place these words on a scale or a continuum.

Harsh meaning	*Reprove*	*Soft meaning*
rebuke,		kindly intent
reprimand		to correct
		a fault

4 3 2 1 0 1 2 3 4

By combining these definitions with the word *betimes*, we reach the following fundamental principles:

You might reprove—rebuke or reprimand—and do it with sharpness—curtly, pointedly, severely.

You might also reprove—with kindly intent to correct a fault—and do it with sharpness.

And of course you should do it "betimes"—early, promptly, quickly, at the right season or time.

While the dictionary gives several definitions for the word *sharp* or *sharpness*, in the context of the scripture we are considering it clearly carries the meaning of a pointed, severe rebuke—hence the need for "showing forth afterwards an increase of love toward" the one reproved (D&C 121:43).

And it is most important that one should reprove in this way only "when moved upon by the Holy Ghost." Does the Holy Ghost function in this way? Does He rebuke and reprimand curtly, pointedly, severely? Yes, He does! Read these accounts of "reproving betimes with sharpness."

The angel reproved Laman and Lemuel (see 1 Nephi 3:29).

Nephi reproved his brothers (see 1 Nephi 7:15–16; 1 Nephi 17).

Lehi was chastened by the voice of the Lord (see 1 Nephi 16:25).

The angel spoke to Alma and the four sons of Mosiah (Mosiah 27:11–17).

Samuel the Lamanite spoke to the Nephites (Helaman 13–15).

Impressive are the two accounts of the Savior in the temple with the money changers (John 2:13–17 and Matthew 21:12–16) or the account of Jesus speaking to the scribes and Pharisees (see Matthew 23).

Many more examples could be given as to this feature of the Holy Ghost's works. All of them illustrate what I discovered from defining three words—*reprove, betimes,* and *sharpness.*

The Lord's Definitions

Scattered throughout scriptures are definitions given by the Lord and His prophets. Sometimes the word *is* is accompanied by the word *which*. Other ways of recognizing definitions are the words "I would speak in other words," or simply "in other words."

Consider the following examples:

"For the word of the Lord is truth, and whatsoever is truth is light, and whatsoever is light is Spirit, even the Spirit of Jesus Christ" (D&C 84:45). I mark definitions in my scriptures with an equation symbol "=" placed over the word. You can make these stand out more by the following:

"For the word of the Lord $\overset{=}{\text{is}}$ truth, and whatsoever is truth $\overset{=}{\text{is}}$ light, and whatsoever is light $\overset{=}{\text{is}}$ Spirit, even the Spirit of Jesus Christ" (D&C 84:45).

Word = truth
Truth = light
Light = Spirit (D&C 84:45)
Glory = intelligence
Intelligence = light of truth
Intelligence = light and truth (D&C
    93:29, 36)
Voice = spirit
Spirit = truth (D&C 88:66)
Words = spirit and life (John 6:63)
Rest = fulness of glory (D&C 84:24)

I have listed below some of the most significant definitions given by the Lord. In each of these examples a statement is made, followed by an elaboration on the statement. These explanations can often be identified with the words *is*, or *or*, and the phrase "I would speak in other words."

Reference	Word or phrase	Definition
1 Nephi 10:4	a Messiah	or in other words, a Savior
1 Nephi 10:14	grafted in	come to the knowledge of the true Messiah, their Lord and their Redeemer
1 Nephi 11:25	rod of iron	was the word of God
1 Nephi 11:36	great and spacious building	was the pride of the world
1 Nephi 17:5	Irreantum	many waters
1 Nephi 19:7	trample under their feet	set him at naught and hearken not to the voice of his counsels
2 Nephi 6:13	people of the Lord	they who wait for him
2 Nephi 26:29	priestcrafts are	men preach and set themselves up for a light
2 Nephi 26:30	charity is	love
Alma 18:13	Rabbanah, which is	powerful or great king
3 Nephi 27:13–21	my gospel	the Savior's mission and atoning sacrifice (see chapter heading)
Moroni 7:47	charity is	the pure love of Christ
Moroni 8:17	charity is	everlasting love
D&C 11:24	my rock is	my gospel
D&C 19:11	Eternal punishment is	God's punishment
D&C 19:12	Endless punishment is	God's punishment
D&C 29:30	word of my power is	power of my Spirit
D&C 59:13	fasting may be perfect	joy may be full
D&C 59:14	fasting and prayer	rejoicing and prayer
D&C 84:24	his rest is	the fulness of his glory
D&C 86:2	the field was	the world
	the apostles were	the sowers of the seed
D&C 93:36	the glory of God is	light and truth intelligence

Archaic Word Definitions

The LDS Edition of the King James Version of the Bible has footnotes that explain certain words. Four keys found in the footnotes are explained in the introductory pages of the Bible as follows:

GR: An alternate translation from the Greek.

HEB: An alternate translation from the Hebrew.

IE: An explanation of idioms and difficult constructions.

OR: The word *or* signifies that alternate words follow to clarify the meaning of archaic English expressions.

The Hebrew and Greek entries are usually examples of word definitions. In the *or* and IE entries you will find both definitions and commentaries or explanations. Some of the definitions are archaic words and phrases, and others are alternate translations as indicated. You have already seen the definition of the archaic word *betimes* at the beginning of this chapter. A few examples from the Bible are as follows:

Reference	*Key word*	*Definition*
Genesis 2:18	help meet	Footnote 18b IE a helper suited to, worthy of, or corresponding to him
Genesis 5:29	Noah	Footnote 29a IE Rest, or Repose
Genesis 17:17	laughed	Footnote 17a HEB (also) rejoiced
Exodus 20:8	sabbath day	Footnote 8a HEB stopping, cessation, rest (from labor)
Exodus 12:23	suffer	Footnote 23c OR allow
Exodus 20:11	hallowed	Footnote 11c OR sanctified, or consecrated
I Samuel 10:27	held his peace	Footnote 27b IE ignored them
Matthew 6:9	After this	Footnote 9a IE It is in this way that you ought to pray
John 12:24	corn	Footnote 24a GR grain, seed
1 Cor. 3:16	in	Footnote 16c GR in, within, among

You will find definitions not only in the Bible footnotes but also in the Bible Dictionary. One of the most fascinating Bible Dictionary definitions I have found is the phrase "by and by"[1] (see Matthew 13:21). The definition from the Bible Dictionary is "an English term that in 1611 meant *immediately*. However, in common usage today it has come to mean nearly the opposite." (LDS Bible Dictionary, p. 627.) Applying this archaic definition of the phrase as it appears in Alma 32:42 gives me a new appreciation for the promise of when you can pluck the fruit from the tree, which is the harvest from the experiment upon the word.

While such definitions are rarely found in the footnotes to the triple combination, it contains many archaic words and expressions. Therefore, it is helpful to have a good dictionary nearby when you study scriptures.

An interesting word in scripture whose archaic usage may not always be clear is the word *only*. One synonym or definition of the word *only* is the word *except*. The following references illustrate the word *only* when it apparently means "except":

Reference	Phrase
Mosiah 3:21	"None shall be found blameless before God, except it be little children, only [except] through repentance and faith . . . "
Alma 12:9	"They shall not impart only [except] according to the portion of his word"
D&C 89:13	"And it is pleasing unto me that they should not be used, only [except] in times of winter, or of cold, or famine."
D&C 121:36	"The powers of heaven cannot be controlled nor handled only [except] upon the principles of righteousness."

1. The phrase "by and by" appears 12 times in the four standard works—Matthew 13:21; Mark 6:25; Luke 17:7; 21:9; Alma 32:42; Alma 55:11, 14; 3 Nephi 27:11; Ether 5:1; D&C 63:35; 101:58; JS-M 1:55. In the Bible where this phrase appears it is probably used in its archaic meaning; however, in those references from latter-day scriptures it is not as clear. One could probably build a case for a dual meaning in some of the references.

In scripture study it will sometimes surprise you that when you define a word that is very common, insights and appreciations will come to you. Such was the case for me with the word *kindly* from Doctrine and Covenants 99:6. In this revelation to John Murdock, wherein he was called to preach the gospel, the Lord told him, "It is not expedient that you should go until your children are provided for, and sent up kindly unto the bishop of Zion." I asked myself, how does one send a child *kindly* to his or her bishop? Among other archaic definitions of the word *kindly* in Webster's unabridged dictionary is that of a normal or a natural way. That perhaps would fit the circumstances—the children were not to be rushed and should travel in comfort and be treated with kindness. Another definition is "a gesture of goodwill."

While serving as bishop, I looked forward to interviewing the youth. It was a privilege to be in their presence. I was also thankful to their parents, who sent them to me "kindly"—as a natural, normal course and as a gesture of their goodwill. When our own children went to our bishop for their interviews, they were always "sent up kindly."

Word Origins

Profound insights have come to me through studying a word in its original language, such as in Hebrew or Greek or Latin. But you might say, "I do not speak those languages." Neither do I! But I do speak English, and that is all you need.

Many English words come from German, Latin, and Greek. You have two basic sources to find these meanings: one is a good English dictionary, and the other is a lexicon. In high-quality English dictionaries you will find the history and development of a word (this is called its etymology). In a lexicon you will find words arranged alphabetically in a language, accompanied by the definition of those words. Hebrew and Greek lexicons are extremely valuable. Note how Elder Russell M. Nelson teaches profound truths about home teaching from John 21:15–17 through the use of a Greek lexicon.

> Because the available manuscripts of the New Testament are in
> Greek, additional insight is gained when the words . . . are studied in

the Greek language. . . . The word *feed* comes from the Greek term *bosko,* which means "to nourish or to pasture." The word *lamb* comes from the diminutive term *arnion,* meaning "little lamb."

"[Jesus] saith to him again the second time, Simon, son of Jonas, lovest thou me? He saith unto him, Yea Lord; thou knowest that I love thee. He saith unto him, *Feed* my *sheep*" (v. 16; emphasis added).

In this verse, the word *feed* comes from a different term, *poimaino,* which means "to shepherd, to tend, or to care." The word *sheep* comes from the term *probaton,* meaning "mature sheep."

"[Jesus] saith unto him the third time, Simon, son of Jonas, lovest thou me? Peter was grieved because he said unto him the third time, Lovest thou me? And he said unto him, Lord, thou knowest all things; thou knowest that I love thee. Jesus saith unto him, *Feed* my *sheep*" (v. 17; emphasis added).

In this verse, the word *feed* again comes from the Greek *bosko,* referring to nourishment. The word *sheep* was again translated from the Greek term *probaton,* referring to adult sheep.

These three verses, which seem so similar in the English language, really contain three distinct messages in Greek:
- Little lambs need to be nourished in order to grow;
- Sheep need to be tended;
- Sheep need to be nourished. (*Ensign,* August 1994, p. 16.)

As indicated earlier, many words in the LDS Edition of the King James Version of the Bible that are derived from Hebrew and Greek have synonyms in the footnotes. When a biblical word interests you, look it up in a dictionary or in a lexicon. Some that I have found, which have deepened my love for God and His Son and given me a greater understanding of the gospel in the scriptures, are as follows:

compassion   In the Latin it means "to suffer with" (com=with and passion=suffer). When I read that the Savior said, "I will have compassion upon you" (D&C 64:2), deep feelings of gratitude well up in me.

confirm   In the Greek it means "to strengthen more; to strengthen from on high; to render more firm, set resolutely in a predetermined course." Thus Paul and his companions "confirmed the Churches" (see Acts 15:32, 41; 18:23; see also Mosiah 27:33 and D&C 24:9).

converted   In the Latin it means "to turn around, to transform." The Savior's words to Peter, "When thou art converted, strengthen thy brethren" (Luke 22:32), teach me that before I can help others I must be headed in the right direction. Some may be going in the wrong direction, and to be converted is to turn around and be turned towards God.

just   In the Greek, *just* means "to conform to the law of God." When the scriptures speak of Joseph and Noah being just men (see Matthew 1:19 and Moses 8:27), I am convinced this means they conformed their lives to the law of God in every detail.

reconciliation   In the Latin this word means "to sit again with"—re=again, con=with, and silio=chair, or where we sit or are seated. The doctrine of reconciliation is to be able to sit with God again through the atonement of Jesus Christ (see 2 Corinthians 5:18–21).

In the Hebrew and Greek languages, persons' names often communicated special meanings. Nephi and Lehi, sons of Helaman, remembered the words of their father concerning their names: "Behold, I have given unto you the names of our first parents . . . ; and this I have done that when you remember your names ye may remember them; and when ye remember them ye may remember their works; and when ye remember their works ye may know that it is said, and also written, that they were good. Therefore, my sons, I would that ye should do that which is good." (Helaman 5:6–7.)

Notice the significance of the meaning of the following Hebrew names from the Old Testament as they pertain to the promises made to Abraham (see Abraham 2:6, 9–11 and Genesis 17:4–8):

Abraham—father of a multitude

Sarah—princess; princess of the multitude

Israel—who prevails with God

Joseph—increase; addition

Ephraim—fruitful

The names and title of the Son of God are sacred and holy. Knowing their meaning not only enhances my reverence and respect for Him but it also broadens my knowledge of Him and His divine mission and atonement (see LDS Bible Dictionary, *Christ* and *Jesus*, pp. 633, 713).

Summary

The following list of words and the verses in which they appear are provided so that you can learn their meanings and also gain experience with this scripture study technique of word definitions. Because the meanings of many Hebrew and Greek words are found in the footnotes of the LDS Edition of the Bible, I have primarily included archaic words found in the triple combination.

	Reference	*Word*
Book of Mormon	1 Nephi 8:4	methought
	1 Nephi 11:16	condescension
	1 Nephi 15:18	kindreds
	2 Nephi 2:8	merits
	2 Nephi 12:9	mean
	Jacob 5:13	nethermost
	Mosiah 10:12	wronged
	Mosiah 15:9	betwixt
	Alma 1:15	ignominious
	Alma 26:36	mindful
	Alma 39:9	cross
	Helaman 10:4	unwearyingness
	3 Nephi 24:2	fuller's soap

Doctrine and Covenants	20:75	expedient
	25:14	delight
	33:17	trimmed
	43:8	edify
	60:4	bespeaketh
	121:11	hoar frost
Pearl of Great Price	Moses 6:29	foresworn [foreswear]
	JS-H 1:8	poignant
	JS-H 1:44	musing
	JS-H 1:60	stratagem

8

Visualizing

Framed and hanging on a wall in our home is a statement my wife found that applies to left-handed people. Being left-handed, I value it. "God made a few perfect people; the rest He made right-handed." I know I am not perfect, but I am happy to be a left-handed person.

Some scientists say that being right- or left-handed has to do with hemisphericity or brain dominance, the right side of the brain directing the left side of the body and vice versa. One side is generally dominant. Tests for hemisphericity suggest that people who are right-brain-dominant are more artistically inclined, perhaps more inclined to learn visually as opposed to learning verbally. Left-brain-dominant people have more of a disposition to the sciences—math, physics, and so forth.

Regardless of our brain dominance or hemisphericity, learning visually is important and useful. This certainly applies to the scriptures. Valuable insights and profound truths have come to me when I have visualized the scriptures. When it comes to the scriptures, the oft-quoted adage "a picture is worth a thousand words" carries important meaning.

Words are visual symbols, but in this chapter I am talking about pictures, illustrations, or graphics, with some words to help clarify what is illustrated or visualized. (Throughout this chapter the words *visual* and *illustration* refer to the same technique, and *visualizing* may refer also to generating a mental image.)

Visualizing or illustrating the scriptures involves taking a verse or verses and reducing them to a simple visual or picture. Some visuals will come from one verse, from several verses in the same chapter, or from a series of verses scattered throughout several chapters, or even from books of scripture. For example, when I teach a lesson with a chalkboard available, I draw on the chalkboard what is in the scriptures.

A familiar visual to all Latter-day Saints is that of the First Presidency and the Quorum of the Twelve, based on Doctrine and Covenants 107:21–24.

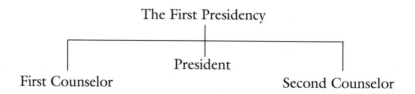

The First Presidency

President

First Counselor   Second Counselor

The Council of the Twelve Apostles

You could continue the illustration of the next priesthood quorums—the quorums of the Seventy, including the Seven Presidents of the Seventy .

A common illustration of a spirit body and a mortal body is a solid line in the form of a body and a dotted line inside the solid line (see D&C 88:15; 93:33; Abraham 3:21–24).

For many years parents, missionaries, and teachers have illustrated the "great plan of the Eternal God" or the "great plan of happiness" as shown in this familiar illustration. Note here that in order to illustrate the plan, you would have to draw upon scriptures found in all four standard works, such as Moses 3:5; 4:1–4; Abraham 3:22–26; Doctrine and Covenants 29:36–37; 76; 137; 138; Alma 42; 3 Nephi 27:13–22; Mormon 9:11–14; and many others.

The Great Plan of Happiness

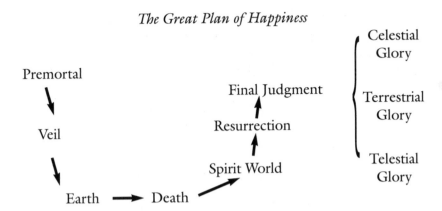

For several years I had the privilege of holding an ecclesiastical calling at the Provo Missionary Training Center and also working there. On the day parents, relatives, and friends brought their missionaries to begin training, one of my assignments was to speak briefly to them and give them an overview and orientation of the training. As part of my concluding remarks, I often asked a missionary to read a verse from the Doctrine and Covenants and while he or she read it, I used a chalkboard to illustrate or visualize what was being read. Each phrase from the scripture is illustrated as follows:

Doctrine and Covenants 84:88

(1) And whoso receiveth you, there I will be also,

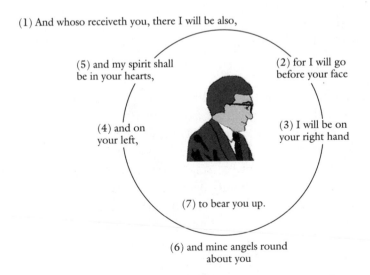

Visualizing these references expands my faith in and love for the Father and the Son, who give their servants such unusual promises and protection. These promises are not idle comments. They are true. My appreciation for this verse is multiplied by simply visualizing it.

Using this same reference from the Doctrine and Covenants and adding a few other references that can also be visualized, the illustration begins to look as follows:

Doctrine and Covenants 76:29

"Wherefore, he [Satan] maketh war with the Saints of God and encompasseth them round about."

Helaman 5:12

"Remember that it is upon the rock of our Redeemer, who is Christ, the Son of God, that ye must build your foundation; that when the devil shall send forth his mighty winds, yea, his shafts in the whirlwind, yea, when all his hail and his mighty storm shall beat upon you, it shall have no power over you."

One of the most helpful insights I have ever received concerning the atonement of Jesus Christ came as a result of visualizing the concepts taught in the scriptures.

The prophet Abinadi testified that Jesus Christ is both the Father and the Son (see Mosiah 15:1–5). Following this explanation, he provided a list of nine truths concerning Christ and His atonement:

"And thus God breaketh the bands of death, [1] having gained the victory over death; [2] giving the Son power to make intercession for the children of men—[3] Having ascended into heaven, [4] having the bowels of mercy; [5] being filled with compassion towards the children of men; [6] standing betwixt them and justice; [7] having broken the bands of death, [8] taken upon himself their iniquity and their transgressions, [9] having redeemed them, and satisfied the demands of justice" (Mosiah 15:8–9).

It is the sixth item that caught my attention. This I have visualized, putting myself in the scriptures. It looks somewhat like this—

God.
Justice comes
from Him. He said
"no unclean thing enters."

Jesus stands
"betwixt"
us and justice.

We are unclean.
We need help.

While reading the Doctrine and Covenants one day, I discovered what might be a possible plea or dialogue from the Savior to His Father on our behalf. With the plea inserted, the visual now looks as follows:

God.
Justice comes
from Him. He said
"no unclean thing enters."

"Listen to him who is the
advocate with the Father,
who is pleading your cause
before him—saying: Father,
behold the sufferings and
death of him who did no sin,
in whom thou wast well
pleased; behold the blood of

thy Son which was shed,
the blood of him whom
thou gavest that thyself
might be glorified;
wherefore, Father,
spare these my brethren
that believe on my name,
that they may come unto
me and have everlasting
life" (D&C 45:3–5).

Jesus stands
"betwixt"
us and justice
and pleads our cause.

We are unclean.
We need help.

With this visual in mind, now substitute your name in verse 5 as follows: "Wherefore Father, spare [your name] that believe[s] on my name, that [your name] may come unto me and have everlasting life." The only way that your name can appear in that verse is through the Redeemer, who "stands betwixt them [or you] and justice" and pleads your cause.

After I have read and studied the scriptures for many years, my visualizing what is written adds new insights. It is as if that verse was not there the last time I read the scripture. This is what happened to me on one occasion. Two gates that are talked about in the scriptures are the gates of hell and the gates of heaven. The gates of hell will not prevail against us if we are built upon the rock and if we keep certain commandments as illustrated below:

Gate of Heaven
Open to all—Helaman 3:28
Narrow gate—2 Nephi 31:9

Must be built upon the Rock
Rock=Christ: Helaman 5:12
Rock=Revelation: Matthew 16:17–18
Rock=My Gospel: Doctrine and
Covenants 11:24

Gates of hell kept shut by our—
Having a broken heart and a contrite spirit—2 Nephi 4:32
Being built on doctrine—3 Nephi 11:39–40
Partaking of the sacrament—3 Nephi 18:13
Being of [the Lord's] Church and enduring to the end—Doctrine
and Covenants 10:69
Testifying of the Book of Mormon—Doctrine and Covenants
17:8
Giving heed to the living prophet—Doctrine and Covenants
21:5–6

When I find scriptures that can be visualized or illustrated, I often put the illustration in the margin of my scriptures. If there is not enough space in the margins, I often prepare the illustration on a piece of paper and glue it in my scriptures as indicated in chapter 4.

Summary

We live in a visual world. Much of what we know and retain has come from visual learning. The scriptures are no exception. Being more aware of the scriptures through visualizing them will deepen your love for and understanding of them.

9

Homilies

Two very good words that describe two scripture activities are *exegesis* and *homiletics*. Exegesis has to do with explaining the meaning of a text. This word is closely related to familiar words such as *exit* or *exodus*, meaning to leave or go out. The definition of exegesis I most prefer is "to draw out the meaning." We desire to draw out meanings from the scriptures. Following is an illustration of exegesis from the Old Testament. The Israelites had been without the written words—the scriptures—for many years. Ezra, the scribe, brought them the holy words from the prophets.

It is in verse 8 that you find an excellent example of exegesis. Note the list of truths illustrating this skill of drawing out the meaning. The readers did three things:

1. They read in the book in the law of God distinctly.	"And Ezra the priest brought the law before the congregation both of men and women. . . .
	"And he read therein before the street . . . before the men and the women; . . . and the ears of all the people were attentive unto the book of the law.
2. [They] gave the sense.	
3. [They] caused them to understand the reading.	"And Ezra opened the book in the sight of all the people; . . . and when he opened it, all the people stood up. . . .

> "So they (1) read in the
> book in the law of God dis-
> tinctly, and (2) gave the sense,
> and (3) caused them to under-
> stand the reading."
> (Nehemiah 8:2, 3, 5, 8.)

Bible scholars will tell you that these three truths relate to a language problem. The scriptures were in an unfamiliar language and had to be translated.

If we look beyond the language issue, these three truths also illustrate what is meant by exegesis. One who draws out these meanings is an exegete. The practice of drawing out meanings is exegetics. In essence the emphasis of this book is exegetics, especially the chapters on principles of substitution, lists, definitions, visualizing, homilies, uniting truths, and story parallels.

While the word *homily* has more than one meaning, for the purposes of this book it means an inspirational catchphrase, a short pithy phrase that has substance and meaning. I prefer to use the idea that homiletics is the practice of identifying a few words that mean a lot. All of us have grown up hearing homilies. For example, in my youth I heard my mother say these two homilies more than any others: "A stitch in time saves nine," and "By the inch life is a cinch, by the yard it is hard." While these two rhyme, most homilies do not.

The scriptures are full of homilies. Finding them is the challenge. Many are personal, meaning that they may have meaning to you but not necessarily to someone else. Usually, however, you can explain to others why you believe it is a homily and most will readily see what you have seen. Because most homilies are seen through spiritual eyes and they are given to you by the Spirit to meet a particular need, I can give you only a few suggestions that have guided me in my search for them.

1. Study, search, and examine words and phrases prayerfully and humbly. Simply reading the scriptures will rarely lead you to see homilies. Perhaps they are hidden the deepest in the scriptures and require much effort to find them.

2. Ignore existing punctuation marks and verse and chapter breaks. These are important, but they also create arbitrary breaks in the flow of ideas.
3. Put periods in a sentence where there are none. This suggestion relates to number two. Putting periods in sentences where there are none causes you to isolate words and phrases.
4. After you have isolated a phrase, ask yourself whether those words express an idea much bigger than the words themselves.

An excellent verse to practice on is one of the most oft-quoted verses in the Book of Mormon. It is Nephi's obedient response to his father concerning the calling to return to Jerusalem to obtain the plates of brass (see 1 Nephi 3:7). Here are a few homilies I have found:

I will.
I will go.
I will go and do.
I will go and do because I know.

I know.
I know that the Lord giveth.

He shall prepare a way.
He shall prepare a way for them.

They may accomplish the thing.

While there are other important truths in this verse, I am looking for a few words that say a lot, that communicate truths far beyond the words themselves.

This verse from the Doctrine and Covenants gives several excellent homilies.

You have been entrusted.
You have been entrusted with these things.
Remember also the promises (D&C 3:5).

I shall never forget the first time I discovered the homily "remember also the promises." My wife and I, along with our six young children, were called to serve a mission in Colombia. As mission president, I left one Thursday morning for a forty-five-minute flight to a city in our mission. I spent the rest of the day interviewing missionaries. From the interviews came a number of concerns that I allowed to disturb me. Discouragement (the absence of courage) would not describe my feelings. I was frustrated and disappointed with what I had found.

We held a less-than-average zone conference. The Spirit simply seemed to be missing. On Saturday and Sunday I conducted a district conference. There were challenges in the district—leaders without goals, poor attendance, lack of punctuality, poor preparation, transgressions, and other concerns. The accumulation of my experiences from Thursday through Sunday afternoon left me feeling low.

I caught a taxi to go to the airport and fly home. I settled into my seat on the plane. Very few people were on the flight, so I had the entire row of seats to myself to sort through what I was feeling.

I took my scriptures in hand and thumbed through the pages, reading here and there. Providentially I came to some verses that will never be the same to me, particularly one phrase, a powerful homily.

Beginning with the first verse of Doctrine and Covenants section 3, I began reading. "The works, and the designs, and the purposes of God cannot be frustrated, neither can they come to naught." I reflected on these words. From Thursday through Sunday, I had come to the erroneous conclusion that the purposes, designs, and works of God were being frustrated, at least in that city.

I continued on with verses 2 and 3. "For God doth not walk in crooked paths." A few missionaries and members certainly were walking in crooked paths. "Remember, remember that it is not the work of God that is frustrated, but the work of men."

Continuing with verse 4: "For although a man may have many revelations, and have power to do many mighty works, . . ." As a mission president I had been made an instrument in the

Lord's hands. I had received revelations and done some good works. Following these words, I found a list that sobered me as mission president. "If he (1) boasts in his own strength, and (2) sets at naught the counsels of God, and (3) follows after the dictates of his own will and carnal desires, he must fall."

But it was in verse 5 that I found the treasure. Everything I had read thus far was only background to one of the most wonderful insights I have ever found in scriptures. "Behold, you [Jay Jensen] have been entrusted with these things . . . ." I paused and lifted my eyes from the page to reflect upon the things entrusted to me: my wife and children, about 100 missionaries, about 6,000 members, 13–14 million nonmembers, a mission, districts, branches, budgets, and so forth. My mind reviewed all that was entrusted to me. "But how strict were your commandments." This did not help my sagging feelings.

Then I came to the next phrase—a homily of homilies to me. What power, what insight, what comfort, what depth of feeling and meaning! *"Remember also the promises"* (D&C 3:5; emphasis added). Four words from scripture had never impacted me as those four did that day. I identified with what Joseph Smith said after he read James 1:5: "Never did any passage of scripture come with more power to the heart of man than this did at this time to mine. I reflected on it again and again." (Joseph Smith—History 1:12.)

I realized that for four days I had focused on nothing but problems. Not once had I stopped to remember the great promises given to me.

"Remember also the promises." I asked myself, "What promises?" The first ones that came to my mind were those in my patriarchal blessing. I had it with me and now reviewed it. My, what promises! I then reviewed the special promises given to me when I was set apart as mission president. I reviewed the promises of the temple. From there I reviewed a number of promises from scripture. My spirits soared! I was inspired.

By this time the plane had landed. As I look back on that short flight home, I realize I was taught from on high. As I walked to the exit to take a taxi home, it seemed as if my feet never touched the ground. From that day until today, my life has been different. All because of four simple words of what I now call a homily—"remember also the promises."

Of Elder Neal A. Maxwell it has been said that he has the gift of creating phrases. I would like to pay tribute to him by saying that he has a gift of identifying homilies. Many, if not most, of the titles to his books are homilies. Evidence that his book titles are homilies is that from one small phrase comes a series of chapters in support of the phrase. Here is a list of some homilies that are titles to his books—

"Of one heart" (Moses 7:18)
"The smallest part" (Alma 26:16)
"All these things shall give thee experience" (D&C 122:7)
"But for a small moment" (D&C 122:4)
"Even as I am" (3 Nephi 27:27)
"Plain and precious things" (1 Nephi 13:28, 29, 40)
"Things as they really are" (Jacob 4:13)
"We talk of Christ, we rejoice in Christ" (2 Nephi 25:26)
"Notwithstanding my weakness" (2 Nephi 33:11)
"We will prove them herewith" (Abraham 3:25)
"That my family should partake" (1 Nephi 8:12)
"Meek and lowly" (Matthew 11:29; Alma 37:33, 34; Moroni 7:43, 44)
"A more excellent way" (Ether 12:11)
"For the power is in them" (D&C 58:28)
"Wherefore, ye must press forward" (2 Nephi 31:20)

An interesting aspect of homilies is that they are very personal. Usually you will have experiences that expand and enrich them—hence their personal nature—or you will find experiences of others that support them. The next two experiences illustrate what I mean.

"Strength such as is not known among men." Missionary work is challenging. All missionaries at one time or another struggle with loneliness, frustrations, and disappointments. (I was going to use the word discouragement, but because it means the absence of courage and because I rarely see this in missionaries, I chose not to include it.) Through their struggles and as they turn to

heavenly powers for help, they grow and develop and become strong, capable, spiritual leaders.

While serving as branch president at the Provo MTC, I saw again and again the fulfillment of the promise in this verse and a homily I have identified in italics. "And at all times, and in all places, he shall open his mouth and declare my gospel as with the voice of a trump, both day and night. And I will give unto him *strength such as is not known among men.*" (D&C 24:12; emphasis added.)

What strengths are most young elders acquainted with? Many come to the MTC familiar with the strength necessary to succeed in competitive sports, school exams, drama, or music. They are acquainted with this kind of strength that comes through their own efforts. This is not to say that young people do not ask for and receive help from Heavenly Father before their missions, because many do. But they may not have come to realize or experience the "strength such as is not known among men."

In his weekly letter to me, his branch president, an elder shared a special experience he had with prayer and fasting. He and his companion were not getting along well. Each was doing some minor things that irritated the other. For example, the elder who wrote me said that his companion was terribly slow. He could not understand how anyone could be so slow. He determined to fast and pray to help solve this challenge.

When it came time for lunch, he accompanied his companion to the cafeteria, thinking he would quietly study and continue his fast while his companion ate. When they arrived, they discovered that the menu was tacos, his very favorite dish. The battle raged inside him. "How can I pass up such a delicious meal? Our problems are not really that bad, are they? Oh my, these tacos look and smell so good. I could fast tomorrow or the next day."

He thought about the purpose of his fast and the benefits and blessings of fasting. He prayed silently in his heart for "strength"—the strength that is not known among men.

In his letter to me he said: "President, I chose to sit there and eat spiritual food instead. I can testify to you, President Jensen, that as a result of my fasting, I have seen two special blessings: one, I have a greater love and understanding for my companion;

and two, my companion and I have been able to talk and help each other to improve in the areas where we need to improve." He experienced strength such as is not known among men.

"*The smallest part which I feel.*" This beautiful homily from Alma 26:16 stirs feelings deep within me every time I read it. For example, I cannot tell you "the smallest part which I [felt]" as my lovely bride and I knelt at the altar in the Manti Temple and were sealed for time and all eternity. I cannot tell you "the smallest part which I [felt]" when I spoke at the funeral of an older brother as heavenly thoughts, feelings, and impressions came from the Comforter to me. Pure intelligence flowed to me. Nor can I tell you "the smallest part which I [felt]" when I baptized and confirmed each of our six children, then ordained the boys to the priesthood, and then went to the temple with each as they either went on missions or married in the temple. And so I could go on with many more examples.

Not only have I experienced it, but I have also seen others enjoy the power of these simple words.

At the Provo MTC, in my initial interview with one young elder he told me of the great love he had for his grandfather, who had practically raised him. As he spoke, I sensed the deep love, reverence, and respect for this grand patriarch. The elder had known little parental love. The parents had divorced when he was a small child.

A few weeks after the interview, I was notified that the grandfather had suffered a heart attack and died. I made arrangements to see the elder alone and there informed him of the death of his grandfather. Tears flowed.

I explained the counsel of the Brethren to encourage missionaries to remain at the MTC and not go home in such circumstances. The decision, however, was his, and I told him we would support him in it. Also, it would have been easy for him to attend the funeral because his home was only a one-hour drive from the MTC. We knelt in prayer, and he said he would think about it and let me know the next day.

The following morning, the elder telephoned me and said that he had decided to remain at the MTC. When he prayed the previous night, he had had the strongest impression that his grandfather would have wanted him to stay. He felt a peace and a comfort never felt before. He could not say "the smallest part which [he felt]" (Alma 26:16). I might also add that he enjoyed a "strength such as is not known among men" (D&C 24:12).

"Arms of safety." One of the sweetest and most tender homilies I have found is "arms of safety" (Alma 34:16). The context in which these words appear is a wonderful discourse by Amulek on the Atonement, particularly the principles of justice and mercy: "And thus mercy can satisfy the demands of justice, and encircles them in the arms of safety, while he that exercises no faith unto repentance is exposed to the whole law of the demands of justice; therefore only unto him that has faith unto repentance is brought about the great and eternal plan of redemption" (Alma 34:16).

The complete homily may be written as "mercy . . . encircles . . . in the arms of safety."

Have you had the responsibility to teach little children abstract truths such as atonement, mercy, justice, and so forth? This homily can help you like few I know in scriptures.

Let me illustrate with an experience as a young father of two children. My wife and I were in the midst of my university education at BYU and I was also working nearly full-time. Work and a full load of classes resulted in long days.

To reduce costs, Lonnie, my wife, sent me off each day with a metal "lunch bucket" with sandwiches and cookies. When I left home each morning our two children, both under age four, saw me leave with the lunch bucket in one hand and my briefcase in the other. When I returned home at the end of the day and drove into the driveway, I got out of the car with my hands full—lunch bucket and briefcase.

Frequently our little ones stood at the front window with their noses pressed against the glass watching and waiting for Daddy to come home. As I walked from the car to the house, they dashed out the front door and ran to me. Each child went for one of my legs, encircling their tiny arms of safety around me and holding on, oftentimes seated on my shoes as I tried to walk a few steps.

Finally I stopped, set aside my briefcase and my lunch bucket, and scooped up a child in each of my arms. Now my arms of safety encircled their tiny bodies and their tiny arms of safety were encircled around my neck. What wonderful safety we enjoyed!

From the driveway I walked into the house, where I sat each child down, and Lonnie's arms of safety encircled me as my arms of safety encircled her.

Arms of safety! Can you visualize this? Arms are very tangible body parts. When they reach out and encircle someone you love, feelings of love and safety are communicated. Using the tangible arms, you can teach intangible truths such as mercy, love, and the Atonement.

Physical arms cannot begin to compare with the glorious experience of being encircled in the Savior's arms of safety. If I understand faith in Jesus Christ, repentance from sin, receiving essential ordinances, and keeping covenants, through the atonement of Jesus Christ I can be made clean. Those who are clean receive mercy. Those who do not exercise faith in Christ and do not repent are exposed—"exposed to the whole law of the demands of justice."

As I think about arms, the word *hugs* comes to mind. Heaven surely has to be a place for hugs. It is not hard for me to visualize being encircled in the arms of safety of God, our Heavenly Father, and receiving a hug from Him. I can visualize the same with the Savior. In addition to these two holy Beings, I can visualize hugs from family members, immediate and extended, and being encircled in the arms of their love.

In one of the hymns of Zion we also sing of this concept: "When life's perils thick confound you,/Put his arms unfailing round you" ("God Be with You Till We Meet Again," *Hymns,* no. 152). From the *Children's Songbook* there is a beautiful verse:

"I wish that his hands had been placed on my head,
That his arms had been thrown around me,
That I might have seen his kind look when he said,
'Let the little ones come unto me.' " ("I Think When I Read
That Sweet Story," *Children's Songbook,* p. 56.)

The scriptures talk not only about "arms of safety" but also about "arms of mercy or love" (see Mosiah 16:12; Alma 5:33; Mormon 5:11; D&C 6:20) and the phrase or homily "encircled about eternally in the arms of his love" (2 Nephi 1:15).

If you were teaching children about the Atonement and mercy, could you illustrate these intangibles of mercy and atonement by arms of safety? I believe you can. A sacred story may also illustrate "arms of safety."

> Away on the Fort Peck Reservation where I was doing missionary work with some of our brethren, laboring among the Indians, seeking the Lord for light to decide certain matters pertaining to our work there, and receiving a witness from Him that we were doing things according to His will, I found myself one evening in the dreams of the night in that sacred building, the temple. After a season of prayer and rejoicing, I was informed that I should have the privilege of entering into one of those rooms, to meet a glorious Personage, and, as I entered the door, I saw, seated on a raised platform, the most glorious Being my eyes have ever beheld or that I ever conceived existed in all the eternal worlds. As I approached to be introduced, He arose and stepped towards me with extended arms, and He smiled as he softly spoke my name. If I shall live to be a million years old, I shall never forget that smile. He took me into His arms and kissed me, pressed me to His bosom, and blessed me, until the marrow of my bones seemed to melt! When He had finished, I fell at His feet, and, as I bathed them with my tears and kisses, I saw the prints of the nails in the feet of the Redeemer of the world. The feeling that I had in the presence of Him who hath all things in His hands, to have His love, His affection, and His blessing was such that if I ever can receive that of which I had but a foretaste, I would give all that I am, all that I ever hope to be, to feel what I then felt! (In *Melvin J. Ballard, Crusader for Righteousness*, pp. 138–39.)

In Joseph Smith—History in the Pearl of Great Price, there are a number of longer homilies. By longer I simply mean that in comparison to the ones above, these are complete sentences, albeit short ones. But each one has a depth of meaning that the concepts teach and communicate much more than the words themselves. In pondering on each example, I confess that I have experienced the same things. Not that I have seen visions, such as the Father and the Son, but I have done and can do what Joseph Smith did. With each one, ask yourself if you can do the same.

verse 12   *"I reflected on it again and again."* I reflect on many scriptures again and again.
"For how to act I did not know." In so many instances, I do not know how to act or what to do. Such is the case when assignments come to reorganize a stake presidency, or when I am called upon to speak with no advance notice. What do we do? We trust in God, as did Joseph. We pray and seek answers.

verse 13   *"I must do."* Like Nephi, "I will go and do" (see 1 Nephi 3:7) and like Joseph, "I must do."

verse 17   *"When the light rested upon me I saw."* This short declaration has so much meaning to me. When the light of the Spirit rests upon me, I see. Jesus laid his hands on a blind man and made him look up. Because of the touch of the Master's hand, he "saw every man clearly" (see Mark 8:25). It will always be so when we are touched by the Light; we will see, and that clearly.

verse 19   *"I was answered."* Like Joseph, think of the number of times you were answered. God does hear and answer our prayers.

verse 20   *"When the light had departed, I had no strength."* This one is similar to the one in verse 17. Just as when the light rests upon me it allows me to see, so it is that when the light departs, I have no strength. After being in the presence of God, Moses learned this well. "And as he was left unto himself, he fell unto the earth. . . . It was for the space of many hours before Moses did again receive his natural strength." (Moses 1:9–10.) But it means so much more than physical strength. In our assignments we can go in our own strength or we can go in the strength of the Lord.

"*I went home.*" Oh my, what a wonderful declaration! Where do we go after we have spiritual experiences? Where is our face directed?

"*I have learned for myself.*" Latter-day prophets have taught that we cannot live on borrowed light.

verse 26   "*I had found the testimony . . . to be true.*" In the process of conversion, all will find the testimony to be true. In this case it was the testimony of James. With each passing day, as I read and study the scriptures, I find other testimonies to be true. It is a never-ending quest.

verse 27   "*I continued to affirm.*" Not only does what we say affirm our belief; so also do our lives affirm it. The scriptures reveal that there are a few things that anger the Lord, one being not opening our mouths (see D&C 60:2–3). Another way of viewing this warning is the failure to continue to affirm what we know.

verse 29   "*I had full confidence.*" Joseph had *full* confidence, not just ordinary confidence. Those who use the priesthood in righteousness enjoy the promise, "then shall thy confidence wax strong in the presence of God" (D&C 121:45).

verse 46   "*I must have no other object in view.*" If there was ever a scripture given that illustrates correct motives, this is it. This verse records Moroni telling Joseph he "must not be influenced by any other motive than that of building [God's] kingdom."

verse 50   "*I obeyed.*" These two words portray the Prophet Joseph Smith like few others. On another occasion he said of himself: "I made this my rule: When the Lord commands, do it" (*History of the Church* 2:170). At the marriage in Cana, Mary said to the servants concerning Jesus, "Whatsoever he saith unto you, do it" (John 2:5). And on and on we could go with a multitude of references in support of these two words, "I obeyed."

verse 61   *"In the midst of our afflictions we found a friend."* This beautiful declaration is one of my favorite homilies. All of us at one time or another encounter afflictions. I also believe that the vast majority of us encounter friends who help us in our afflictions. Among some of our friends are parents, brothers, sisters or other family members. Others are literally companions and associates who stand by us to lift, strengthen, and help. Friends I have found are in the scriptures—prophets and Apostles, ancient and modern. One of my best friends is my patriarchal blessing. But above all my friends are the Father and the Son and the Holy Ghost. No one can be of more help than they when we find ourselves in the midst of afflictions.

Marking Homilies in Scriptures

When I first discovered that homilies exist in the scriptures, I underlined them. But underlining them did not allow me to distinguish them from other truths I underlined, therefore I adopted the practice of enclosing them in quotation marks. Whether they are long ones or short ones, they begin and end with quotation marks. In those few instances where two homilies overlap in the same verse, I use different colored pencils—red and blue.

Behold, you have been entrusted with these things, but how strict were your commandments; and "remember also the promises" which were made to you, if you did not transgress them (D&C 3:5).

" "I will go" and do" the things which the Lord hath commanded, for " "I know" that the Lord giveth" no commandments unto the children of men . . . (1 Nephi 3:7).

The homilies cited thus far are single phrases, each one developed, illustrated, and expanded by experiences. Each homily may also be united to other scriptures where related truths are found. Connecting these ideas is explained with greater detail in chapter 10, "Uniting Truths."

Summary

There is power in the word of the Lord! That power is clearly seen in short sermons or sermonettes that I call homilies. As you prayerfully read and study and search the scriptures, you will find more and more of these short phrases laden with meaning. They will be drawn upon as sources of wisdom, strength, and courage as you face the trials and challenges of life. They will become centerpieces of talks and lessons. They will adorn your thoughts. They will bless your life.

10

Uniting Truths

Most of what we know about the doctrines of the restored gospel does not come from one verse or from one chapter. These truths are found scattered throughout all four standard works. Important doctrines concerning the Godhead, the Fall and the Atonement, the plan of redemption, the three degrees of glory, temple ordinances, infant baptism, the scattering and gathering of Israel, and many, many more are found in more than one of the standard works and are united into complete truths.

Perhaps an analogy will help. I love classical music, especially the major symphonies of great composers. I marvel at the full, complete sounds of many instruments orchestrated and joined to produce beautiful music. Each instrument plays a unique function and sound and contributes as directed by the conductor. So it is with the scriptures. As I study, I become a conductor seeking to bring forth from the scriptures various truths, orchestrated into symphonies of truth and light. Chapters and verses from all four standard works can be joined together in harmony and beauty in the same way that the music conductor draws music from his orchestra.

For example, many children in Primary learn the Articles of Faith, the first one being, "We believe in God, the Eternal Father, and in His Son, Jesus Christ, and in the Holy Ghost" (Articles of Faith 1:1). While this is a beautiful, simple declaration of our belief, it is but the beginning of what we know about God, as is illustrated by uniting the verses that follow.

A scriptural declaration about the nature of the Father, the Son, and the Holy Ghost is: "The Father has a body of flesh and bones as tangible as man's; the Son also; but the Holy Ghost has not a body of flesh and bones, but is a personage of Spirit" (D&C 130:22). Continuing on about the Father, we know that He is "the Father of spirits" (Hebrews 12:9). We also know something of His attributes. "Believe in God; believe that he is, and that he created all things, both in heaven and in earth; believe that he has all wisdom, and all power, both in heaven and in earth; believe that man doth not comprehend all the things which the Lord can comprehend" (Mosiah 4:9).

Alma taught us more about these attributes or characteristics. "We must come forth and stand before him in his *glory*, and in his *power*, and in his *might, majesty,* and *dominion*, and acknowledge to our everlasting shame that all his *judgments* are *just*; that he is *just* in all his works, and that he is *merciful* unto the children of men, and that he has all *power* to save every man that believeth on his name and bringeth forth fruit meet for repentance (Alma 12:15; emphasis added).

In *Lectures on Faith*, the writers and teachers pointed out that God has all knowledge, faith or power, justice, judgment, mercy, and truth (see *Lectures on Faith* 4:4–10). He is all of that and much more.

These holy attributes of God can be studied throughout all four standard works and cross-referenced.

Linking or uniting ideas in scriptures is a wonderful journey through the scriptures, each verse repeating an idea or adding to or complementing previous ones. In truth, it is a never-ending quest. It is an orchestration of light and truth from all four standard works resulting in a symphony of truth, harmony, and beauty.

Nearly all conceptual lessons published in Church manuals that draw upon the four standard works are illustrations of uniting scriptures. Likewise, almost all talks given in our meetings, especially those given by General Authorities, are excellent examples of how to unify scriptures.

The Savior Unified Scriptures

When the adversary confronted the Savior at the beginning of His ministry, Jesus responded to each of the three temptations with a scripture, each one building on the other into a unified whole. In the Sermon on the Mount, Jesus cited Old Testament scriptures and unified them to teach that the Law of Moses was about to be fulfilled (see Matthew 5:21–48). Near the end of His mortal ministry, the Savior accompanied two disciples on the road to Emmaus, and while they walked, "beginning at Moses and all the prophets, he expounded unto them in all the scriptures the things concerning himself" (Luke 24:27). How long this took and what references He cited we do not know, but that He selected a theme and united the scriptures written about Him into a meaningful whole is clear. He knew how to unify the scriptures.

The Savior followed this same pattern when He visited the Americas. Jesus commanded them to search the prophets and "when [he] had said these words . . . he . . . expounded all the scriptures unto them which they had received." And "when Jesus had expounded all the scriptures in one, which they had written, he commanded them that they should teach the things which he had expounded unto them." (3 Nephi 23:6, 14; see also 3 Nephi 26:1–3.)

Unifying Through Footnotes

Footnotes assist us in the quest for unity. Gospel scholarship, doctrinal clarifications, and personal applications are among some of the results of following footnotes in the scriptures. As pertains to unifying ideas, footnotes lead the reader directly to other references and to the lists of references found categorized in the Topical Guide, the Bible Dictionary, and the index to the triple combination.

An example of a footnote wherein one verse adds to or clarifies another is as follows: the Apostle Paul taught that "where the Spirit of the Lord is, there is liberty" (2 Corinthians 3:17). The superscript "b" precedes the word *Spirit* and leads to the footnote "17b Alma 61:15, TG God, Spirit of." The reference from Alma speaks of "the Spirit of God, which is also the spirit of freedom which is in them" (Alma 61:15).

In the event that you are reading in Alma, the process can be reversed by following the footnote provided (see footnote "b" for Alma 61:15). If additional information is desired, the reader can turn to the Topical Guide and study the topic "God, Spirit of." Although the footnote "17b" in 2 Corinthians 3 does not include the suggestion to go to the topic "Freedom," hopefully as a student of the scriptures you will prayerfully search the topic on your own if it interests you.

Footnotes can lead the reader to:

1. A single reference that gives doctrinal or historical support. Sometimes the idea expressed in the cross-reference is readily apparent because key words are repeated; other times it is more conceptually designed and the reader has to look beyond the words themselves and find the concept(s) hidden in the words. For example, 1 Nephi 1:1 superscript "d" leads you to footnote "d," which leads you to an excellent related reference in Enos 1:1.

2. Two or more verses that state the same idea or word and related concepts. Often the footnote references clarify and complement the source verse. All verses cited may be similar to that expressed in 1 above. The superscript "c" in 1 Nephi 3:7 leads you to footnote "c" and illustrates references that are conceptual and a repetition of the word *prepare.*

3. The Topical Guide or the Bible Dictionary where you will find additional information and help. The Topical Guide helps in two ways—(1) it serves as a concordance, and (2) it provides topics.

A concordance serves to help the reader find additional references where the same or similar words are repeated, whereas the topical entries provide conceptual information. When the Topical Guide appeared in the Bible for the first time, students of the scriptures learned that some subjects are not identified by the same words in the Bible text—such as *Attributes of God.* The reader can turn to the different Bible words used to discuss this topic: *see* God, Eternal Nature of; God, Knowledge about; Godliness. If the reader looks up God, Eternal Nature of, he will find a helpful concordance of key words, and also many doctrinally illuminating scriptures. Note these helpful concordance entries under the entry *Scripture*: (*see* also Scriptures, Lost; Scriptures, Preservation of; Scriptures, Study of; Scriptures, Value of; Scriptures, Writing of; Scriptures to Come Forth; Dictionary: Scripture).

The Bible Dictionary "has been designed to provide teachers and students with a concise collection of definitions and explanations of items that are mentioned in or are otherwise associated with the Bible" (LDS Bible Dictionary, p. 599).

4. Other scripture study helps that include alternate language translations, difficult idioms or word constructions, and other resources and explanations.

Because of space limitations and also to promote spiritual self-reliance, it was not possible nor intended to include every possible reference in the footnotes and other study aids. Consequently, students of the scriptures should mark and annotate their own set of scriptures and unite and orchestrate truths they find. The longer I study and mark my scriptures, the more it becomes apparent that most of the markings in them now are reflections of truths I have found, both aided by existing study aids and independent of them.

Latter-day Scriptures and the Bible

In our uniting ideas, some related passages are found in different volumes of scriptures and others are found within the same volume. Perhaps one of the most important concepts to emphasize is the way in which latter-day scripture clarifies or amplifies Bible passages. Often the uniting of these ideas involves only two passages of scripture. Latter-day scripture is one of the best sources from which to clarify truths in the Bible.

Jesus taught his disciples about the first and second comforters. "Jesus answered and said unto him, If a man love me, he will keep my words: and my Father will love him, and we will come unto him, and we will make our abode with him" (John 14:23). The Prophet Joseph Smith clarified this verse as follows: "John 14:23—The appearing of the Father and the Son, in that verse, is a personal appearance; and the idea that the Father and the Son dwell in a man's heart is an old sectarian notion, and is false" (D&C 130:3).

Another example is the parable of the wheat and the tares in Matthew. The sequence of the harvest in the New Testament is to gather first the tares, then the wheat (see Matthew 13:30). In the Doctrine and Covenants the sequence of the harvest is reversed: first gather the wheat, leaving the tares to be burned (see D&C 86:7). Although a small change, it is significant in doctrine, for the clarification in latter-day scriptures points out the sequence of the gathering as going forth in The Church of Jesus Christ of Latter-day Saints.

When the Savior commissioned the Twelve Apostles just prior to His ascension, He told them: "Go ye into all the world, and preach the gospel to every creature. He that believeth and is baptized shall be saved; but he that believeth not shall be damned." (Mark 16:15–16.) A very important addition is given to this commission in the following revelation to the Prophet Joseph Smith: "Go ye into all the world, preach the gospel to every creature, *acting in the authority which I have given you*, baptizing in the name of the Father, and of the Son, and of the Holy Ghost. And he that believeth and is baptized shall be saved, and he that believeth not shall be damned." (D&C 68:8; emphasis added.)

The italicized words "*acting in the authority which I have given you*" are not found in the Gospel of Mark but are included in the revelation to Joseph Smith.

The parable of the ten virgins in Matthew 25 states that "all those virgins arose and trimmed their lamps" (Matthew 25:7). The foolish virgins did not have oil. This account from Matthew is enriched by the information in Doctrine and Covenants 33:17: "Wherefore, be faithful, praying always, having your lamps *trimmed and burning, and oil with you*, that you may be ready at the coming of the Bridegroom" (emphasis added).

Alma taught simple, plain doctrine as to one's knowing the mysteries of God that adds to and clarifies the Savior's explanation of why He spoke in parables (compare Alma 12:9–11 with Matthew 13:13–17).

The Savior's command in the New Testament to "love the Lord thy God with all thy heart, and with all thy soul, and with all thy mind" has added to it in latter-day scriptures the important command "and in the name of Jesus Christ thou shalt serve him" (D&C 59:5).

The above are but a few of the many illustrations of a combination of two verses, where one clarifies or adds to the other. Also, it is interesting to note that in each example cited, beginning with the references about the comforters, a footnote reference is included to guide you to the verse that clarifies the first reference.

Not only can two verses be formed to teach important truths, but a series of verses can link concepts within all four standard works.

Unifying Ideas in All Four Standard Works

The value of unifying truths within the scriptures is illustrated with the principle of obedience. Often while touring a mission, I share with missionaries three significant references, and each one complements the others. Because there are no printed footnotes to support these truths, I make my own marginal notes and comments.

The first is "He that keepeth his commandments receiveth truth and light" (D&C 93:28). But what is truth and light? This is answered with the second reference: "For the word of the Lord is truth, and whatsoever is truth is light, and whatsoever is light is Spirit, even the Spirit of Jesus Christ" (D&C 84:45). With every commandment we keep, we receive light and truth or the Spirit. The third truth is "And that wicked one cometh and

D&C 84:45–46; 130:19
"He that keepeth his commandments receiveth <u>truth and light</u>" (D&C 93:28).

taketh away light and truth through disobedience" (D&C 93:39). Failure to keep commandments results in a loss of light and truth or the Spirit.

The following sequence about faith, prayer, and the will of God illustrates the power that can come from unifying truths from the scriptures. To preserve these truths in my own copies of the scriptures, I write the next scripture reference in the margins of my scriptures (see the illustration).

"And that wicked one cometh and taketh away <u>light and truth</u> through disobedience, from the children of men, and because of the tradition of their fathers" (D&C 93:39).

"And Christ hath said: If ye will have faith in me ye shall have power to do whatsoever thing is <u>expedient in me</u>" (Moroni 7:33). See Moroni 7:26

Moroni 7:33	Faith in Christ leads to power to do *whatsoever is expedient.*
Moroni 7:26	Whatsoever we ask the Father, *which is good,* believing we shall receive we shall receive.
D&C 88:64–65	Whatsoever we ask the Father in the name of Christ and it is expedient, it shall be given, *but if not expedient* for us, it shall turn into condemnation unto us.
D&C 29:6	Whatsoever we ask in faith, *being united in prayer,* we shall receive.
Mormon 9:21	Whoso believes in Christ, *doubting nothing,* whatsoever he shall ask the Father in the name of Christ shall be granted.
Moses 6:32	The Lord will do as *seems to Him good.*
D&C 11:14	We shall know all things that *pertain to righteousness,* if in faith we believe we shall receive.
Mark 9:23	All things are possible *to him that believes.*

D&C 50:29–30   If we are purified and cleansed from sin, what we ask in the name of Jesus shall be done. But, *it shall be given* what we shall ask.

Helaman 10:4–6   Because of serving with unwearyingness, without fear, not seeking his own life, and seeking the Lord's will and keeping His commandments, Nephi was made mighty in word, deed, faith, and works. All things were to be done according to his word. In light of the above, he would *not ask anything contrary to the will of God*. The final result was *power*.

One of the central themes of the Book of Mormon is the gathering of Israel; indeed, the coming forth of the Book of Mormon is the sign to indicate the beginning of the gathering. Book of Mormon writers never lost sight of this important doctrine. It begins with the title page:

> Which is to show unto the remnant of the House of Israel what great things the Lord hath done for their fathers; and that they may know the covenants of the Lord, that they are not cast off forever—And also to the convincing of the Jew and Gentile that JESUS is the CHRIST.

In the latter days "shall the fulness of the gospel of the Messiah come unto the Gentiles, and from the Gentiles unto the remnant of our seed" (1 Nephi 15:13). When Moroni came to Joseph Smith and instructed him concerning the plates, he said "that the fulness of the everlasting Gospel was contained in [them]" (JS-H 1:34). "And at that day shall the remnant of our seed know that they are of the House of Israel, and that they are the covenant people of the Lord; and then shall they know and come to the knowledge of their forefathers, and also to the knowledge of the gospel of their Redeemer, . . . wherefore they shall come to the knowledge of their Redeemer" (1 Nephi 15:14).

In summary, note the sequence of ideas and how they build on each other in a unified whole. Because the printed footnotes do not include this sequence of ideas, handwritten marginal notes and references preserve these truths in my copies of the scriptures.

Principle	*Source*
• Three purposes of the Book of Mormon help us know about Israel, covenants, and the divinity of the Savior.	Title page
• The fulness of the Gospel goes to the Gentiles and then to Nephi's seed who are of the House of Israel, a covenant people.	1 Nephi 15:13
• The Book of Mormon contains the fulness of the gospel.	JS-H 1:34
• With the Book of Mormon, Nephi's seed shall know they are of Israel and of the covenant and that Jesus is the Christ, as stated in the purpose statement from the title page.	1 Nephi 15:14

On one occasion while I was reading, a truth from Doctrine and Covenants 17:8 concerning the gates of hell opened up to me. The following truths are united into a meaningful concept to illustrate the power that comes from unifying scriptures. There are two gates:

1. The gate to heaven is open to all (Helaman 3:28). It is a narrow gate (2 Nephi 31:9; 33:9). Nephi called this gate "the gates of thy righteousness" (2 Nephi 4:32).
2. The gates of hell are broad and wide (3 Nephi 27:33; D&C 132:25). The Greek word for gates in Matthew 16:18 indicates the larger sort, as opposed to a smaller one. These gates are open and ready to receive those who choose to pursue a course that leads through them. Of those who enter or pass through them, the scriptures say that these gates prevailed.

What was most interesting to discover was that in each reference where the phrase "gates of hell" appears, the Lord teaches us how we can avoid having the gates of hell prevail. These truths are as follows:

1. Have a broken heart and contrite spirit and the gates will remain shut (2 Nephi 4:32).
2. Be built upon my doctrine, my rock, repent, believe in Christ and be baptized, and the gates of hell shall not prevail (3 Nephi 11:38–40; D&C 33:11–13).
3. Administer the sacrament, meaning that if you are a priesthood leader you must do it precisely as the Savior instituted it; and if you are a member, you should partake of it as instructed, which is, repent, be baptized, and then partake of the sacrament in remembrance of the body and blood of Christ. If you do this, when the floods and rain and wind come you will be built upon the rock, and the gates of hell will not open to you (3 Nephi 18:1–13).
4. Be of the Lord's Church and endure, and the gates of hell shall not prevail (D&C 10:69).
5. Do these last commandments (meaning that you testify of the Book of Mormon) and the gates of hell shall not prevail against you (D&C 17:8).
6. Do these things—give heed to the words of the living prophet with all diligence and faith (D&C 21:4–6). Note also the two other promises that come from doing "these things"—the Lord (a) will disperse the powers of darkness and (b) will cause the heavens to shake for your good.

In summary:

1. Have a broken heart and contrite spirit (also, these are the qualifications to be baptized).
2. Build upon doctrine, fundamental principles, and the rock of revelation, and exercise faith, repent, and be baptized.
3. Renew the baptismal covenant properly.
4. Be an "enduring" member of the Church.
5. Testify of the Book of Mormon.
6. Follow the living prophet.

By our doing these six things, the gates of hell shall not prevail in our lives. I have listed them, along with the scripture references, on a blank page in my scriptures.

One of the most difficult but useful exercises in my life was an assignment from the President of the Quorum of the Twelve to the members of the Seventy to reduce in writing the plan of salvation to a single page. What I thought would take a few hours to accomplish turned out to take much, much longer. I suppose I could reproduce it here, but then you would not learn what I learned in the exercise. Consequently, I leave the thought as an invitation to unify and simplify into one single-spaced typewritten page what you know to be the key elements about the premortal life, the Creation, the fall of Adam and Eve, the atonement of Jesus Christ, mortal death, the resurrection, final judgment, and kingdoms of glory.

To conclude this chapter, I share some insights about the Resurrection that came to me and that illustrate unifying scriptures around a single topic. It all came about as a result of an opportunity to speak in a sacrament meeting.

Because it was Easter Sunday, I spoke on the Atonement. One of the scriptural passages I quoted was Helaman 14:17–18, which teaches that the Resurrection brings a condition of repentance. To me this is a significant principle of the gospel. Were it not for the Resurrection and the reality that we will live again and be brought before God and Christ to be judged of our works, there would be no justification for repentance.

I continued to ponder and study this concept, reviewing in my mind what else the Resurrection brings or does, and concluded the following thoughts on the Resurrection as they pertain to man (note: my preferred reference is in italics):

The Resurrection:

1. Overcomes the Fall and its effects (see *1 Corinthians 15:22;* Mosiah 16:7–8; Helaman 14:15–18; D&C 138:19; Moses 6:59).
2. Brings the condition of repentance (see *Helaman 14:17–18*).
3. Unites the body and spirit into an immortal soul, never to

be separated (see 2 Nephi 9:12–13; *Alma 11:45*; Mormon 6:21).

4. Brings a restoration of all attitudes, attributes, qualities, and gifts acquired in mortality (see *Alma 41:13, 15*; D&C 130:18–19).

5. Restores us to the presence of God to be judged of our works (see Mosiah 16:10–11; Alma 5:15; *11:43–44; 42:23*).

6. Brings a fulness of joy to those who receive a celestial, exalted body, but when spirit and element are separated they cannot enjoy such a fulness (see *D&C 93:33–34*).

Summary

Unifying truths, doctrines, and principles from the scriptures is probably one of our most common study activities. We are often aided by existing study aids, such as footnotes and cross-references. As we immerse ourselves more and more in them, we will create more and more of our own. The examples in this chapter have been included as illustrations of the processes involved.

11

Revelation and Scripture Study

Few commands or invitations are repeated more in the scriptures than to ask, seek, search, or knock. Elder Boyd K. Packer has reminded us that "an important key is turned when we go through the formality of stating our desires to Him who can grant them" (*Teach Ye Diligently*, p. 12). Asking for light and truth concerning truths in the scriptures will be answered with revelations from God. We regularly pray for or seek guidance in life and the important decisions and needs we have. It is just as essential that we do the same when we read, study, and search the scriptures.

The focus of this chapter is on seeking revelation concerning what we study and then valuing it by writing the thoughts, insights, and impressions that come. Some are brief and, if desired, can be written in the margins of your scriptures. Longer ones require more space and can be written in a journal or in a notebook.

Some people have found it helpful to keep two journals, one that is a journal of their life history and a second that includes impressions and insights from the study of the scriptures. Others keep their life history and scripture insights in the same journal.

While reading and studying the scriptures, ask for and seek revelation. Then when impressions, insights, and understanding come, all of which is revelation, write it. For some of the insights I note the date in the margin of my scriptures, and from that date I can turn to that entry in my journal and review the truths learned. How sad when revelation comes and we either fail to recognize it or do not value it sufficiently to write it! Much of what is contained in the four standard works consists of the insights and impressions revealed to prophets and others by the power of the Spirit.

Many revelations contained in the four standard works were responses prophets wrote to questions generated by their study of the scriptures. Examples from the Doctrine and Covenants, some of them being clarifications of biblical passages, are sections 13, 18, 57, 74, 76, 77, 86, 113, 130, and 138.

An illustration of the process of studying, pondering, and searching, of receiving revelation and writing it, is found in Doctrine and Covenants 138, which is known as the vision of the redemption of the dead. It is important to emphasize that what we will read is what President Joseph F. Smith wrote, an account of the process as well as the insights (I have added emphasis to key words that describe the process):

v. 1	President Joseph F. Smith *sat* in his room *pondering* the scriptures. For some, posture may not be important, but there is merit in making the comment that while lying down may be relaxing, it can lead to drowsiness and sleepiness. President Smith *sat*, supposedly having eliminated distractions and becoming focused on the scriptures. Also, it is important to state the obvious—he had the scriptures open. Although the record does not state this, he must have had pen and paper handy to write what he was thinking, seeing, and feeling.
vv. 1–4	He *reflected* upon a specific topic, in this case the atoning sacrifice of the Savior. As he thought on this doctrine, having *engaged* his mental process, his "mind reverted to the writings of the apostle Peter," a specific scripture reference.
v. 6	He "*opened* the Bible and *read*" the verses that came to his mind. He added that "as I read I was greatly *impressed*" with specific verses, which he then quoted. Humility is an important prerequisite to being impressed by something. Also, there is value at times in writing or copying scripture. Words often stand out and impressions come.

v. 11 As he *pondered* over the written word, "the eyes of my understanding were opened, and the Spirit of the Lord rested upon me, and I saw" the vision of the redemption of the dead.

v. 28 President Smith "*wondered* at the words of Peter." This time the reference was from 1 Peter 3:19–20, which he quoted. Also, to wonder is to ponder, think, analyze, ask questions, marvel.

v. 29 "And as I *wondered*, my eyes were opened, and my understanding quickened."

A summary of the key words outlining the process is to—
- Sit.
- Open the scriptures.
- Ponder.
- Reflect on something specific.
- Engage the mind.
- Open other scriptures.
- Be impressed and ponder more, and ask, "is there more?"
- Wonder, express gratitude, and ask, "is there more?"
- Write what is learned.

This marvelous revelation captures as effectively as any recorded revelation from the four standard works the process of studying scriptures, pondering their content, seeking light and truth, and then writing what one has learned.

Often when impressions and insights come, it is helpful to have a tape recorder nearby because they come so fast that the slow process of writing is an obstacle.

When these powerful truths come as answers to prayer, it is important to express gratitude in prayer. At the same time, one should not overlook the question, "Father, is there more?" While I was in the company of one member of the Quorum of the Twelve, he shared with me his experience with this process. While he was studying a particular scripture, impressions began to come. He wrote the truths he received and expressed gratitude for the same; then he asked in prayer whether there was more. More came. Again he expressed gratitude and repeated the same question, and still more came.

What he learned that day I do not know, nor did I ask. Such is the case with many of the revelations and insights we receive; they are sacred and only for us. If we prove unworthy of the trust of our Heavenly Father with personal revelation, He may not grant more until we prove our trustworthiness. We must learn to keep these confidences. A scripture illustration of this truth is found in the miracle of Jesus healing the blind man in Bethsaida. After the healing Jesus "sent him away to his house, saying, Neither go into the town, nor tell it to any in the town" (Mark 8:26).

The keeping of confidences is illustrated by Saul in the Old Testament (see 1 Samuel 9 and 10). He had gone with his servant in search of asses that had strayed. At the same time, Samuel was searching for the first king of united Israel. The Lord created what I sometimes call a divine rendezvous—two individuals came together unbeknown to each other and each accomplished their purposes. Here Samuel found the first king of Israel, and Saul found his asses. Prior to their departure from each other, Samuel placed his hands upon Saul's head and anointed him to be king. Apparently this was a private encounter—no one else was present.

When Saul returned home, his uncle asked where he had been. Saul answered, "To seek the asses: and when we saw that they were no where, we came to Samuel. And Saul's uncle said, Tell me, I pray thee, what Samuel said unto you. And Saul said unto his uncle, He told us plainly that the asses were found. But of the matter of the kingdom, whereof Samuel spake, he told him not." (1 Samuel 10:14–16.) He knew how to keep the matter of being anointed king confidential. Keeping some personal insights and impressions confidential will help to ensure that the Lord will trust us with more.

Revelation and Scripture Marking

In chapter 4 we discussed scripture marking. A key principle taught was that scripture marking is a reflection of our study habits. Scripture marking is also a reflection of the revelations, insights, and impressions we receive.

Shading and underlining generally reflect what stands out to you. What stands out are the feelings and insights that came to you while studying, searching, and pondering the scriptures. If someone were to examine my copies of the scriptures, it would be easy for them to see my insights and revelations by what I have marked and annotated.

Those who go beyond the shading and marking and begin annotating verses with comments, insights, and impressions are capturing revelations that come to them.

12

Story Parallels

Scattered throughout the four standard works are stories, some of which parallel our day in unique ways. All are valuable in that they teach history, values, truths, principles, doctrines, and applications. However, not all scripture stories contain all the elements that readily and easily transfer to conditions and situations in our day. Some stories are simply more relevant and transfer more easily than others.

To transfer easily and with relevance to our day, the following elements are normally present in the story from the scriptures:

1. A story line is followed.
2. The story line has a definite beginning and ending.
3. Phrases or principles from the story illustrate eternal truths. (The phrases often fit the criteria of a homily—see chapter 9.)
4. These phrases depict truths applicable both in former times and in our day.
5. It is as easy to bridge these truths beginning in former times as from our day.

I was first introduced to this concept by Leland Andersen, a master teacher and a professional inservice trainer in the Seminary and Institute program of the Church. I was in my second year of teaching in the seminary program. We were informed that Brother Andersen would be visiting our classes that day. Also, we knew that you only had to invite him to say a few things to the students and he would take a good portion of the class time. Such was the case when he came into my classroom that morning. It was an Old Testament class. He took a piece of chalk in hand and began with the story of David and Goliath. Within seconds he had the class's full attention, but more important, I knew I was watching a master teacher at work as he taught me how to make story parallels in the scriptures.

Later I came to know this concept as bridging the gap, illustrated as follows:

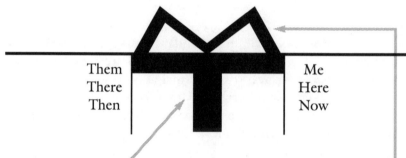

The challenge is to build a bridge between the "them" (prophets and people in the past), the "there" (where they lived), the "then" (during their time), and the "me," who lives in the "here" and the "now," in this day and age and time. The "M" and the "T" are as one, creating a natural bridge.

Brother Andersen took us to 1 Samuel 17 and bridged the gap. He pointed out the setting for the conflict between the Israelites and the Philistines and for Goliath's invitation. He identified the four phrases that parallel our day with the corresponding truths we face.

Verse	Phrases from the Scriptures	Parallels to Our Day
29	Is there not a cause?	We become involved in many causes in our day. What are some?
39	I have not proved them (the armor).	What armor have I proved?

| 45 | I come to thee in the name of the Lord. | We go and come in the name of the Lord. How does a priesthood holder go and/or come in the name of the Lord? |
| 46 | That all the earth may know that there is a God in Israel. | Our purpose is to help others know there is a God in Israel. |

Brother Andersen developed each of the four principles by emphasizing the key phrases. He began by helping students to see causes in which they engaged or would do so, such as helping and serving someone, serving a mission, marrying worthily in the temple, and others. One of the greatest causes of mortality is to "seek to bring forth and establish the cause of Zion" (D&C 6:6). He pointed out wrong causes such as terrorism and gangs, the drug culture, immorality, and so forth.

Next he discussed with the students the armor of God that helps us in the Lord's causes (see Ephesians 6:11–18 and D&C 27:15–18). Also, he pointed out that David could not go forward wearing armor that did not fit him. We cannot live on borrowed light. We have to have our own testimony, our own knowledge, our own armor.

The third phrase, "I come to thee in the name of the Lord," was developed by Brother Andersen's comments that we have been baptized into The Church of Jesus Christ of Latter-day Saints, and we have taken upon ourselves the name of Jesus Christ. We are His covenant children. We go and come in the name of the Lord. The teacher skillfully involved the young men in the class by helping them to see that as Aaronic Priesthood holders, each week they officiate over the sacrament *in the name of the Lord*. As home teachers they always go *in the name of the Lord*.

He concluded with the fourth phrase "that all the earth may know that there is a God in Israel." Here he talked about motives. Why do we do what we do? Why do we become involved in the causes in which we become involved? Why do young men and women serve missions? Why do we marry in the temple? An excellent discussion followed, with the focus on leading others to know that there is a God in Israel. He is Jehovah, the Savior and Redeemer of the world. Our mission is to lead others to know Him, love Him, serve Him, and become perfected in Him.

Watching a master teacher develop these four points opened a door to scripture study, that of searching for parallels in stories.

Identifying Story Parallels

Identifing story parallels is primarily a spiritual matter. As you read and study the scriptures, be prayerful. Pray often. Pray before you begin studying, and, of course, following a study session. Pause at times as you study; express gratitude for what you are learning and ask for additional light and truth. When you are reading stories from the scriptures, pray to find parallels. Most of those that I have found came through prayer, study, searching, pondering, and listening to impressions.

I have to constantly remind myself to study scriptures, which is more than reading them. As you study and search for story parallels, the technique of homiletics described in chapter 9 may help you—put periods in a sentence where there are none. This causes you to isolate phrases. As you isolate them, ask yourself if the isolated words and phrases have meaning for the "them-there-then" and for the "me-here-now." These isolated phrases that I call homilies, when placed together, form a story and become the key elements of the story parallels. (Before reading the story parallels below, you may want to review again the chapter on homilies.)

Another way that I have found story parallels is sitting at the feet of master teachers, as was my good fortune with Brother Leland Andersen, and watching and listening as they unfold them. Other master teachers are General Authorities. Carefully and prayerfully watching them, listening to their scripturally based messages, and studying their words will lead you to see story parallels.

A Story Parallel from the Old Testament

For me the Old Testament is one of our richest volumes of scriptures with story parallels. My set of scriptures contains more marked and annotated examples from that volume than any other.

One of the most complete illustrations is that of the calling of Saul to be the first king of united Israel (see 1 Samuel 10). To me this chapter is without equal in leadership principles from the *them-there-then* that can be applied to the *me-here-now*.

Verses	*Them-There-Then Principles*	*Me-Here-Now Principles*
1	"The Lord hath anointed thee to be." In this case it was being captain or king over united Israel.	The Lord anoints us to be a teacher, a leader, to whatever calling we currently have in the Church.
6	1. "The Spirit of the Lord will come upon thee." 2. "Thou shalt prophesy with them." 3. "Thou shalt be turned into another man." These three promises are given to every person who has been anointed to be a leader.	The same three promises pertain to us today, who also have been anointed to be. 1. The Spirit of the Lord will come upon us. 2. We shall prophesy with others. (Prophecy here may refer to bearing testimony of Jesus—see Revelation 19:10.) 3. We shall be turned into better men and women.
7	"Do as occasion serve thee; for God is with thee."	Because God is with us in our callings, we can "do as occasion serve us" or be guided in the very moment (see D&C 46:2).
8	"I come to . . . shew thee what thou shalt do."	A leader not only tells but shows what to do.
9	"God gave him another heart."	God gives another heart to us as we faithfully fulfill callings.
10–13	"Is Saul also among the prophets?"	Is [name of a person] also a bishop, a president, or whatever the calling? Can good come from *that* family?
14–16	"But the matter of the kingdom . . . [Saul] told him not."	But of the matter of the interview with your leader, you told them not. Keep confidences!
22	"He [Saul] hath hid himself among the stuff."	Feelings of inadequacy cause us to "hide" from callings.

Verses	Them-There-Then Principles	Me-Here-Now Principles
24	"See ye him whom the Lord hath chosen, that there is none like him among all the people."	See ye him who has been called to that position. There is none like him in all the class, quorum, ward, stake, and so forth.
25	"Every man to his house."	Every man and woman to their home, where they learn and live the gospel.
26	"A band of men, whose hearts God had touched."	Members of the class, quorum, ward, stake whose hearts God had touched.
27	"Children of Belial despised him . . . and brought him no presents."	Some despise the new leader and bring no presents, such as a broken heart and a contrite spirit.
27	"But [Saul] held his peace."	Leaders seek peace and forgiveness, not vengeance and reprisals.

By our uniting the *them-there-then* with the *me-here-now* in the above account from 1 Samuel, the following principles are taught:

1. Callings come from the Lord (verse 1).
2. Spiritual gifts come with every calling (verses 6–8).
3. The adversary, either directly or through others' challenges, questions and opposes callings we receive, at times involving family members (verses 10–13).
4. Learn to keep confidences (verses 14–16).
5. Be humble (verse 22).
6. Sustain leaders in their callings (verses 24–25).
7. Allow God to touch your heart concerning the calling of your leaders. Obtain a testimony that those who preside over you are divinely called (verse 26).
8. Recognize that there will always be those who challenge, question, oppose, or fail to support their leaders with presents such as time, talents, means, finances, and other resources (verse 27).

9. Wise leaders seek peace for those over whom they preside, even when opposition comes.

A Story Parallel from the New Testament

The next illustration comes from the healing of the blind man (Mark 8). I remember discovering these parallels from the homily "and [he] saw every man clearly" (Mark 8:25). When I discovered this truth for the first time, I studied and searched more and found the other principles and truths that form the story parallel. Each one led me to appreciate and love the truth that I can see every man clearly. I thought how wonderful it would be if I could see every man clearly, beginning with my wife and children. With the day-to-day challenges of home living, work, Church callings, and other responsibilities, I knew that seeing clearly would be a great blessing.

To learn what made it possible for this man to see clearly I began with verse 22 and discovered a simple, beautiful story parallel.

Verses	*Them-There-Then Principles*	*Me-Here-Now Principles*
22	"They bring a blind man unto [Jesus]."	The physically and spiritually blind are brought to Jesus or His leaders.
22	"They besought him to touch him."	The reason why the blind are brought to Him is so that He can touch them with His love, His doctrine, His Spirit, and His power.
23	"And he took [him] by the hand, and led him out of the town."	The spiritually and physically blind are taken by the hand with tenderness and led into the privacy of a room in a home, into a bishop's office, or into a friend's home, where they can feel and enjoy the touch of the Master's hand.

Verses	Them-There-Then Principles	Me-Here-Now Principles
23	"He put his hands upon him."	Hands are placed on us by worthy priesthood holders, representing the hands of the Savior.
24, 25	"He looked up. . . . He *made* him look up." (Emphasis added.)	Look up. Look to God and live. Look to God and see. Some need encouragement.
25	"He put his hands again upon his eyes."	Hands are placed on us again and sometimes again and again.
25	"He was restored and saw every man clearly."	People are restored and see every man, woman, and child clearly. Also, they see leaders clearly as true servants of the Lord.
26	"Nor tell it to any."	Once healed by the touch of the Master's hand tell it not, unless authorized by the Spirit—not in firesides, books, or talks. These miracles are sacred.

In summary the key elements from the *them-there-then* and the *me-here-now* in this story are as follows:

1. The spiritually and physically blind are brought to Jesus and to His representatives.
2. Those so afflicted are brought to Jesus so that He can touch them in some way.
3. Those needing help are led to a private place where they can be alone.
4. Jesus touches us in some way—with doctrine, ordinances, counsel, His Spirit, love, and oftentimes by His servants here on earth.
5. The blind are to look up, and sometimes with encouragement from others.
6. Some people require more than one touching.
7. Those so touched will see every man clearly.

8. Keep confidential the sacred experiences coming from the touch of the Master's hand.

The mission of The Church of Jesus Christ of Latter-day Saints is to invite all to come unto Christ and be perfected in Him (see D&C 20:59; Moroni 10:32). Everything we teach—every doctrine, every commandment, every program—all are intended to lead us to the Savior where we can be touched by Him.

To many Latter-day Saints a familiar poem or story is "The Touch of the Master's Hand." It is the account of an auction wherein a violin was offered, and was bid for at a very low price. But then an old gentleman came from the back of the room, tuned the violin, adjusted the bow, and skillfully played a sweet and beautiful melody. The auctioneer then offered the violin again, and it sold at a much higher price. What was the difference? It was the touch of the master's hand. The writer concludes with the message that the souls of men can likewise sink low and get out of tune, but when touched by the Master's hand they produce that which is sweet, noble, and pure.

A Story Parallel from the Book of Mormon

A Book of Mormon illustration of story parallels comes from Mosiah 26, the account of Alma dealing with transgressors in the Church.

In this Book of Mormon example the exact words or phrases from the verses in the *them-there-then* column are not included. Instead, I have isolated general principles. The principles are based on the verses, and the exact wording can be identified if desired. This practice can also be applied to the illustrations from the Old and New Testaments (see above). Note that the principles were identified in the summaries following each table (see above).

Also, notice in the *me-here-now* column that an application is made to the relationship between a bishop and a stake president. The people involved could be a parent and child, a stake president and a General Authority, and so forth.

Verses	*Them-There-Then Principles*	*Me-Here-Now Principles*
1–5	Transgressors and unbelievers were found in the Church.	Transgressors and unbelievers are in the Church today.
6–10	Leaders were troubled and asked Alma for help, who went to Mosiah to seek the answer.	Leaders are troubled and ask help from their leaders, for example, a bishop asks the stake president for help.
10–12	Mosiah left the matter in Alma's hands.	The stake president leaves the matter in the bishop's hands.
13	Alma was still troubled and turned to the Lord for help.	The bishop is still troubled, and he turns to the Lord for help.
14–32	The Lord revealed the answer to Alma.	Through faith and prayer, the bishop receives the answer from the Lord.
33–39	Alma wrote the answer and implemented the counsel given.	The bishop may write the impressions he receives and implement them.

Much can be said about the important principle of spiritual self-reliance. The tendency today is to look to others for the causes and solutions to all of our problems, but as illustrated in the account from Mosiah 26, and as taught by latter-day prophets, we are not to shift to others the responsibility to find the answers to our problems. Others may assist us in a variety of ways, but the responsibility remains with us as individuals.

A Story Parallel from the Doctrine and Covenants

Other than the history in which the Doctrine and Covenants came forth and from which many stories come, few stories are found in the actual text of this volume of scripture. However, there is a parable from which we can draw parallels (see D&C 101:47–55).

Verses	*Them-There-Then Principles*	*Me-Here-Now Principles*
47	"And what need hath my lord of this tower?"	They questioned a commandment.
48	"[They] consulted for a long time."	This is what some call "analysis paralysis." While they were consulting, no action was taken.
48	"Seeing this is a time of peace."	A mortal's uninspired view led them to their limited vision and their narrow conclusion.
49	"For there is no need of these things."	With their limited mortal perspective, they came to their mortal conclusion.
50	"While they were at variance."	In their analysis and their mortal view, they argued and could not agree.
50	"They became very slothful."	Questioning, mortal views, arguments, resulted in slothfulness—no action.
50	"They hearkened not unto the commandments of their lord."	The final result was disobedience.
51	"The enemy came by night and broke down the hedge; . . . destroyed their works, and broke down the olive trees."	The enemy is the destroyer. He is the prince of darkness. He seeks to destroy us and the Father's work.
54	"The watchman upon the tower would have seen the enemy while he was yet afar off."	Wise and inspired leaders would have seen the enemy and would have given us the doctrines, principles, and programs to conquer the enemy.

What a marvelous message for our day and time! Prophets, seers, and revelators have never allowed such to happen in our day. They have seen the enemy and have taught us the only sure path, the gospel of Jesus Christ. Only as we keep our eyes on the prophets, seers, and revelators and follow their counsel will we conquer the enemy of our souls.

A Story Parallel from the Pearl of Great Price

Finally, an illustration of story parallels comes from Joseph Smith-History. The specific setting is the translation of the Book of Mormon. Joseph Smith and those who assisted him were under constant pressure to protect the plates and the translation work. Enemies abounded. Efforts to steal the plates persisted. In the midst of these historical events, a story parallel develops for us in our day.

Verses	Them-There-Then Principles	Me-Here-Now Principles
61	Excitement, rumor, and a thousand tongues circulated falsehoods about Joseph.	Excitement, rumors, and falsehoods may be circulated about us.
61	Persecution became intolerable.	Persecutions today may seem intolerable.
61	They were very poor, and the persecution heavy upon Joseph, Emma, and others.	Poverty and persecution seem to go hand in hand.
61	"In the midst of our afflictions we found a friend."	In the midst of our afflictions we will find a friend—a parent, a family member, a leader, or a teacher. Other friends are our Father in Heaven, the scriptures, and doctrine.
61	The friend [Martin Harris] came and gave Joseph fifty dollars to assist Joseph and Emma on their journey.	Friends come to us and give, perhaps not money but love, kindness, counsel, to assist us on our journey through life.

This story parallel was found when I saw the homily "in the midst of our afflictions we found a friend." All else is an outgrowth of this simple, beautiful phrase. All of us have afflictions, but if we exercise faith, be patient, and do our best, deliverance will come by means of friends.

Summary

Story parallels begin with stories in the scriptures or from the events surrounding them. As you read and study them, you will see a word, a phrase (homily), a principle that seems as real today as it did in the past. As you continue your prayerful study, other principles will become apparent. As you put the principles together, you will begin to bridge the gap between the prophets and people who lived in the past—*them-there-then*—and the *me-here-now*. Perhaps this is what Nephi meant when he said that he "did liken all scriptures unto us, that it might be for our profit and learning" (1 Nephi 19:23), and furthermore, by so doing we are treasuring up His words (see Joseph Smith-Matthew 1:37).

13

Promises of the Living Prophets

Harold B. Lee:

Are you brethren continually increasing your testimony by diligent study of the scriptures? Do you have a daily habit of reading the scriptures? If we're not reading the scriptures daily, our testimonies are growing thinner, our spirituality isn't increasing in depth. We ourselves, must be studying the scriptures and have a daily habit. (Regional Representatives' Seminar, December 12, 1970, p. 10)

Bruce R. McConkie:

I think that people who study the scriptures get a dimension to their life that nobody else gets and that can't be gained in any way except by studying the scriptures. There's an increase in faith and a desire to do what's right and a feeling of inspiration and understanding that comes to people who study the gospel—meaning particularly the standard works—and who ponder the principles, that can't come in any other way. (*Church News,* January 24, 1976, p. 4)

By regular, systematic study of the standard works we can go a long way toward keeping in a course that will please the Lord and further our own eternal progression. In this way we can gain for ourselves peace and satisfaction and happiness in this life and have a hope of eternal life in the world to come. (In Conference Report, October 1959, p. 51)

Our tendency—it is an almost universal practice among most Church members—is to get so involved with the operation of the institutional Church that we never gain faith like the ancients, simply because we do not involve ourselves in the basic gospel matters that were the center of their lives.

We are so wound up in programs and statistics and trends, in properties, lands, and mammon, and in achieving goals that will highlight the excellence of our work, that we "have ommitted the weightier matters of the law." And as Jesus would have said: "These [weightier things] ought ye to have done, and not to leave the other undone." (Matthew 23:23.) . . .

However talented men may be in administrative matters; however eloquent they may be in expressing their views; however learned they may be in worldly things—they will be denied the sweet whisperings of the Spirit that might have been theirs unless they pay the price of studying, pondering, and praying about the scriptures. (Regional Representatives' Seminar, April 2, 1982, pp. 1, 2)

Spencer W. Kimball:

All through the scriptures every weakness and strength of man has been portrayed, and rewards and punishments have been recorded. One would surely be blind who could not learn to live life properly by such reading. (*The Teachings of Spencer W. Kimball,* p. 133)

The years have taught me that if we will energetically pursue this worthy personal goal [of scripture study] in a determined and conscientious manner, we shall indeed find answers to our problems and peace in our hearts. We shall experience the Holy Ghost broadening our understanding, find new insights, witness an unfolding pattern of all scripture; and the doctrines of the Lord shall come to have more meaning to us than we ever thought possible. As a consequence, we shall have greater wisdom with which to guide ourselves and our families, so that we may serve as a light and source of strength to our nonmember friends with whom we have an obligation to share the gospel. (*The Teachings of Spencer W. Kimball,* p. 135)

I find that when I get casual in my relationships with divinity and when it seems that no divine ear is listening and no divine voice is speaking, that I am far, far away; if I immerse myself in the scriptures, the distance narrows and the spirituality returns. I find myself loving more intensely those whom I must love with all my heart and mind and strength, and loving them more, I find it easier to abide their counsel. (*The Teachings of Spencer W. Kimball,* p. 135)

I find that all I need to do to increase my love for my Maker and the gospel and the Church and my brethren is to read the scriptures. I have spent many hours in the scriptures during the last few days. I prescribe that for people who are in trouble. I cannot see how any-one can read the scriptures and not develop a testimony of their divinity and of the divinity of the work of the Lord, who is the spokesman in the scriptures. (*The Teachings of Spencer W. Kimball,* p. 135)

George Q. Cannon:

I have noticed . . . that where the people of God pay attention to the written word, and cherish and observe the written word, they are always better prepared to hear the oral instructions of the servants of God . . . they have greater interest in seeking to obtain instructions than they have when they are careless about the written word of God. (In Conference Report, October 1897, p. 38)

Joseph Smith:

Search the scriptures—search the revelations which we publish, and ask your Heavenly Father, in the name of His Son Jesus Christ, to manifest the truth unto you, and if you do it with an eye single to His glory, nothing doubting, He will answer you by the power of His Holy Spirit. You will then know for yourselves and not for another. You will not then be dependent on man for the knowledge of God; nor will there be any room for speculation. No; for when men receive their instruction from Him that made them, they know how He will save them. (*Teachings of the Prophet Joseph Smith,* pp. 11–12)

Marion G. Romney:

I feel certain that if, in our homes, parents will read from the Book of Mormon prayerfully and regularly, both by themselves and with their children, the spirit of that great book will come to permeate our homes and all who dwell therein. The spirit of reverence will increase; mutual respect and consideration for each other will grow. The spirit of contention will depart. Parents will counsel their children in greater love and wisdom. Children will be more responsive and submissive to the counsel of their parents. Righteousness will increase. Faith, hope, and charity—the pure love of Christ—will abound in our homes and lives, bringing in their wake peace, joy, and happiness. (*Ensign,* May 1980, p. 67)

Howard W. Hunter:

Those who delve into the scriptural library, however, find that to understand requires more than casual reading or perusal—there must be concentrated study. It is certain that one who studies the scriptures every day accomplishes far more than one who devotes considerable time one day and then lets days go by before continuing. Not only should we study each day, but there should be a regular time set aside when we can concentrate without interference. (*Ensign,* November 1979, p. 64)

Boyd K. Packer:

If your students are acquainted with the revelations, there is no question—personal or social or political or occupational—that need go unanswered. Therein is contained the fulness of the everlasting gospel. Therein we find principles of truth that will resolve every confusion and every problem and every dilemma that will face the human family or any individual in it. ("Teach the Scriptures," Address to Religious Educators, October 14, 1977, p. 5)

Works Cited

Clark, J. Reuben. *Man, God's Greatest Miracle*. Salt Lake City: Deseret Book Co., 1956.

Children's Songbook. The Church of Jesus Christ of Latter-day Saints, 1989.

Kimball, Spencer W. *Faith Precedes the Miracle*. Salt Lake City: Deseret Book, 1972.

___. *The Teachings of Spencer W. Kimball*. Edited by Edward L. Kimball. Salt Lake City: Bookcraft, 1982.

McKay, David O. *Gospel Ideals*. Salt Lake City: *Improvement Era*, 1953.

Melvin J. Ballard—Crusader for Righteousness. Salt Lake City: Bookcraft, 1966.

Morrison, Alexander B. *Visions of Zion*. Salt Lake City: Deseret Book, 1993.

Packer, Boyd K. *Teach Ye Diligently*. Salt Lake City: Deseret Book, 1975.

Reynolds, George, and Janne M. Sjodahl. *Commentary on the Book of Mormon*. 6 vols. Salt Lake City: Deseret Book, 1955–1965.

Smith, Joseph. *Teachings of the Prophet Joseph Smith.* Selected by Joseph Fielding Smith. Salt Lake City: Deseret Book, 1976.

Smith, Joseph F. *Gospel Doctrine.* Salt Lake City: Deseret Book, 1966.

Taylor, John. *The Gospel Kingdom.* Selected and arranged by G. Homer Durham. Salt Lake City: Bookcraft, 1964.

Young, Brigham. *Discourses of Brigham Young.* Selected by John A. Widtsoe. Salt Lake City: Deseret Book, 1946.

Index